HARVEST OF DEATH

HARVEST OF DEATH

A Detailed Account
of the Army of Tennessee
at the Battle of Franklin

Carey C. Jewell

ILLUSTRATED

Exposition Press
Hicksville, New York

FIRST EDITION

© 1976 by Carey C. Jewell

All rights reserved, including the right of reproduction in whole or in part, in any form or by any means, electronic or mechanical, including photocopying, recording, or by any information storage and retrieval system, without permission in writing from the Publisher. Inquiries should be addressed to Exposition Press, Inc., 900 South Oyster Bay Road, Hicksville, N.Y. 11801.

ISBN 0-682-48654-X

Printed in the United States of America

To my wife, Nancy

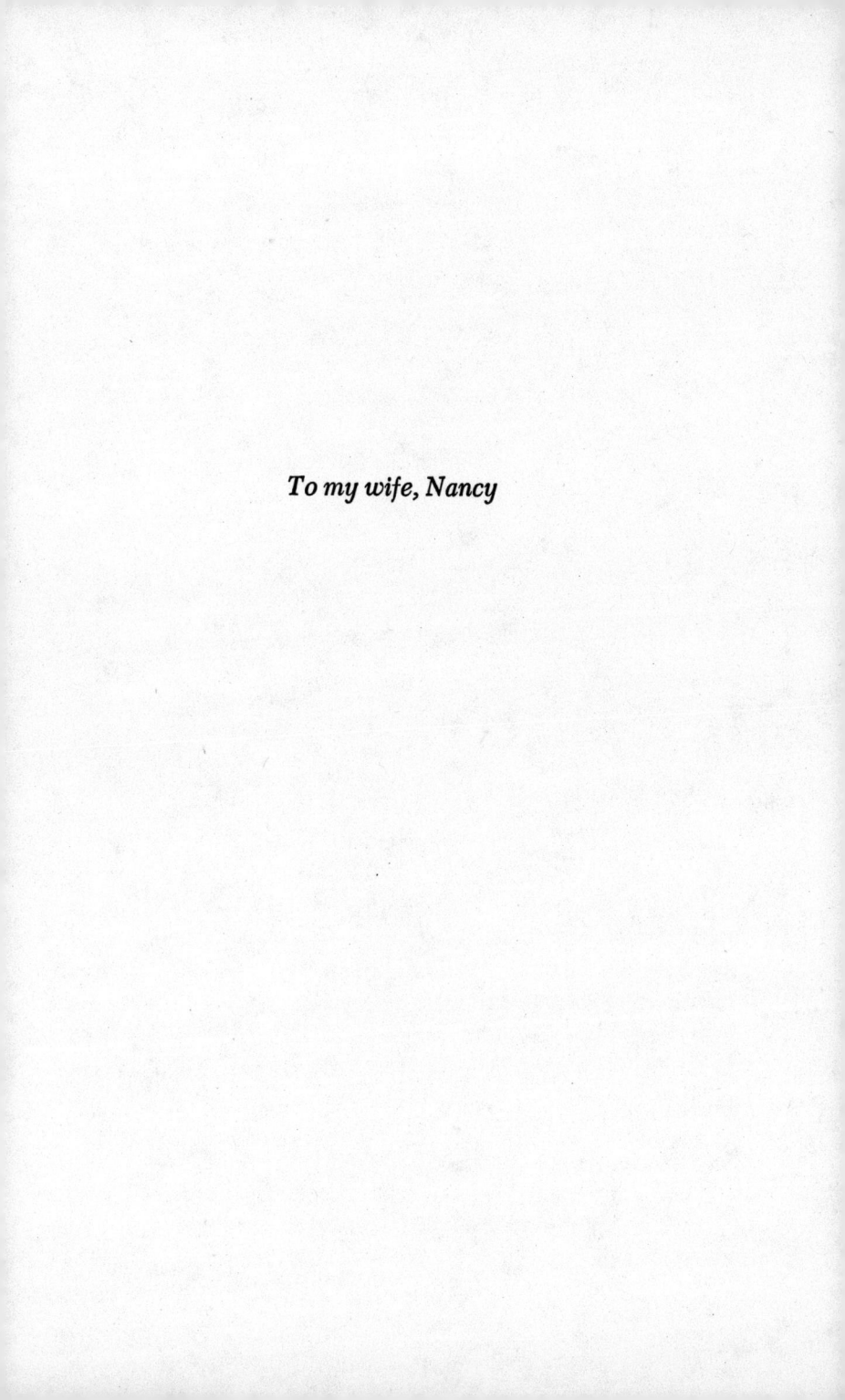

Contents

Preface   9

I. The Beginning   13
II. The Invasion   17
III. Pulaski to Spring Hill   25
IV. Franklin   39
V. Carter Hill   45
VI. On the Right at Franklin   53
VII. The Cavalry   62
VIII. The Last Attacks   67
IX. The Aftermath   73

Appendix   77

Bibliography   87

Preface

"The battle of Franklin, for its proportions, was one of the grandest of the war," wrote Thomas B. Van Horne in his official *History of the Army of the Cumberland*. For here was fought one of the bloodiest battles of the war.

General Isaac B. Sherwood, a Union officer wounded in the battle, in his book, *Memories of the West*, stated:

> It was the fiercest death grapple of all battles on either continent. The final day was Appomattox, four months after Franklin; but Appomattox was not a battle. It was an event. Four months before Appomattox the black curtain of destiny had fallen on the vast stage of human grief and woe amid the lurid lights of flashing guns. The epochal date was April, 1865, but the forces that made that date possible were marshalled on the green hills around Harpeth river. At midnight on the battlefield of Franklin, the finger of destiny was lifted, pointing the road to Appomattox.

Colonel Cassius E. Merrill, a Confederate in the battle and later a prominent Nashville journalist, memorialized the role played by general officers:

> Most of our battles from Virginia to Texas were fought by private soldiers, the generals trolling along "just to have it said," but Franklin was the general's own,

both in conception and execution. Franklin was no battle storm, but a cyclone, rather, which struck and seared the earth and left it red with blood and vocal with groans of dying men.

The Union commander in charge of the battle line, Gen. Jacob D. Cox, wrote in his book, *The Battle of Franklin:*

Hood had more men killed at Franklin than died on one side in some of the great conflicts of the war where three, four, or even five times as many men were engaged. His killed were more than Grant's at Shiloh, McClellan's in the Seven-days' battle, Burnside's at Fredericksburg, Rosecrans's at Stone's River or at Chickamauga, Hooker's at Chancellorsville, and almost as many as Grant's at Cold Harbor.

The battle of Franklin signaled the end of all hope for the success of the Confederate cause and completely wrecked the second major field army of the Confederacy: The Army of Tennessee. It was at Franklin that the army died. Even Pres. Jefferson Davis in his memoirs conceded that the battle of Franklin was the most frightful of the entire war. The battle of Franklin has been called the "Gettysburg of the West."

HARVEST OF DEATH

Chapter I

The Beginning

Was it a major change of Confederate strategy with which Gen. William T. Sherman had to deal in the early days of November, 1864? Sherman could not understand the movements of his foe under General Hood. Their two armies had been maneuvering over the pine lands of Georgia the past month, with Hood evading major battles.

Hood's army had entered Alabama, from where he was threatening to invade Tennessee. General Sherman wired his superior, Gen. U. S. Grant, asserting that regardless of Hood's movements, he did not think that Hood was going to enter Tennessee. Sherman reassured Grant further by his promise to detach elite units back to defend Tennessee.

Sherman was obsessed with the desire to make a march through Georgia to the sea and was doing his utmost to encourage General Grant about Hood so permission would be granted for the march. Grant wired Sherman, desiring to know which units would be dispatched and who would command the forces.

Sherman notified Grant that the Fourth Corps, 12,000 men under Gen. David S. Stanley, would report to Nashville, plus Gen. John M. Schofield's Twenty-third Corps of 10,000 men. Also, Sherman continued, two divisions totaling 12,000 men under Gen. Andrew J. Smith would be ordered to Nashville from Missouri. Sherman stated that this would leave him an army of 60,000 seasoned men to march through Georgia.

The commander of the forces for the defense of Tennessee would be Maj. Gen. George H. Thomas. Thomas was a Southerner by birth, but despite his Southern birth, he stayed with the Union. As a colonel he led a brigade in the Shenandoah Valley. In August, 1861, he became a brigadier general in Kentucky, winning the battle of Logan's Crossroads, January 19, 1862. He was promoted to major general in Buell's army. Thomas fought well at the battle of Stone's River but won his real fame at the battle of Chickamauga. His division held the vital Snodgrass Hill against the victorious Confederates, and he earned the title "Rock of Chickamauga." Thomas commanded the forces that carried Missionary Ridge in the battle of Chattanooga. At the battle of Peachtree Creek, Thomas and his men had borne the main Confederate drive. Thomas was the natural choice for command in Tennessee.

General Stanley's 12,000 troops proceeded by rail to Tullahoma, Tennessee. Unloading his troops and equipment, General Stanley marched to Pulaski, seventy-three miles south of Nashville.

Several days later, Gen. John M. Schofield's Twenty-third Corps was transported by rail to Tullahoma with orders to follow Stanley to Pulaski. General Smith was having transportation problems in Missouri and was delayed in joining Thomas at Nashville.

General Thomas's main concern at the time was his cavalry. The only cavalry available consisted of the two mounted divisions of Gen. John T. Croxton and Gen. Edward Hatch. These forces were detailed to patrol the Tennessee River and, if possible, delay Hood's crossing. General James H. Wilson, who had just been assigned to Thomas, undertook the task to increase the blue cavalry.

Wilson was graduated from West Point in 1860 and served as a topographical engineer in Virginia early in the war. During the Vicksburg campaign, he was promoted to brigadier general of volunteers in 1863. In the spring of 1864 he commanded a division in Gen. Phil Sheridan's corps in the Army of the Potomac, during the campaign to Petersburg. In October, 1864, as a major general, he was given command of the cavalry of the Military Division of the Mississippi.

General Stanley was at Pulaski awaiting the arrival of Schofield. Stanley's seasoned lot of well-trained troops was busy throwing up breastworks and felt, in the event Hood attacked Pulaski, that they could repel him without Schofield's command. However, General Stanley did not share his troops' feelings; he was anxious for Schofield to arrive.

John Schofield had spent valuable time with a part of his command at Johnsonville trying to catch the rebel-raider Forrest. Forrest and his troopers had destroyed vast military stores at Johnsonville and were gone when Schofield arrived. Schofield and his footsore troops marched to Nashville.

Resting briefly at Nashville, Schofield marched his command to Pulaski, arriving there on November 13. Schofield, since he was department commander, assumed command of Stanley's force. This gave a total of 22,000 veteran fighters at Pulaski to impede Hood's movements.

Schofield was born in New York and was graduated from West Point in 1853. At the outbreak of war he was chief of staff to General Lyon and in November, 1861, was promoted to the rank of brigadier general of volunteers. He headed the Army of the Frontier in Missouri from October, 1862, to April, 1863, becoming major general before he was made commander of the Department of the Missouri. In February, 1864, he took over the Army of the Ohio, one of the three armies under Sherman in the campaign to Atlanta.

Schofield respected Hood, and he felt that Pulaski was not a good site from which to give battle against the hard-fighting machine Hood commanded.

General Wilson, in Nashville, was attempting to build a cavalry force of 12,000 troopers. He wired Washington about the lack of horses. Secretary of War Stanton was so harried by wires from Wilson that he overrode law and cries of protest with an order to seize every horse south of the Ohio. Wilson obeyed. He even took draft horses from the streetcars, plus trick horses from the circus in Nashville. He was determined to get mounts for his troops and show the rebel Forrest that the blue cavalry could fight.

General Sherman wired Grant from Georgia that he was prepared to march and was pleased with the preparations that Thomas had made in Tennessee.

On November 16, 1864, Sherman left Atlanta with his 60,000 troops for the Atlantic. The "March to the Sea" had begun. His policy for Georgia was to be a scorched-earth campaign. The march would be virtually unopposed except by a few regiments of Georgia state troops and elements of rebel cavalry under Gen. Joe Wheeler. Sherman knew, as he rode alongside his marching columns, that the success or failure of the march would depend upon General Thomas. If Hood defeated Thomas, Sherman knew that his army and perhaps the war itself would be lost.

Chapter II

The Invasion

On September 1, 1864, the Army of Tennessee, commanded by Gen. John Bell Hood, retreated from Atlanta. For the past two months Hood had struck at Sherman in bloody sallies but had failed to break Sherman's death grip upon the city.

The Confederacy was shocked by the news that Atlanta had fallen to Sherman. So heavy was the shock and the storm of criticism that President Davis hurried to examine the situation in Hood's army. Davis arrived at Hood's headquarters at Palmetto, southwest of Atlanta, on September 25. He left Palmetto on September 27, with the understanding that if Sherman moved south of Atlanta, Hood would follow him.

General P. G. T. Beauregard, the department commander, met Hood at Gadsden on October 21. Beauregard was concerned why Hood had moved his army into Alabama. Here General Beauregard received shocking news. Hood announced that he was planning to invade Tennessee. Beauregard had objections and some misgivings to the plan. However, after spending the better part of two days discussing it, he thought that Hood might succeed if he moved fast.

On October 22, Hood advanced to Guntersville; from there he marched to Decatur. Again Hood failed to inform his superior of a change in plan. He seemed to regard Beauregard almost as a figurehead.

Hood informed Richmond that the approaches at Decatur were too heavily guarded for him to cross and that he would have to move down the river to Courtland. Arriving at Courtland on October 30, Hood discovered that he would not have ample provisions for his campaign.

The army was in sad need of equipment and clothing. Hood, in order to acquire the sorely needed supplies, moved his footsore force from Courtland to Tuscumbia.

The Army of Tennessee began crossing the Tennessee River by pontoons on the tenth of November near Tuscumbia but stopped at Florence on the opposite side. Hood was still waiting for his provisions. The vital supplies of rations and ammunition were delayed due to torn railroad track by Union raids.

The South was losing her zeal; the army had no way of knowing that she was digging her grave with the long delay at Florence. The splendid force that had fought the Union army around Atlanta was becoming the ghost of an army, a band of shadows, with regiments a hundred strong.

The badly needed supplies arrived, but now torrential rains made the roads impassable for wagons. In all, three precious weeks were wasted.

By November 21, with rain still falling, the army pressed northward into Tennessee over the muddy roads. The troops were in good spirits despite the delay and steady downpour of rain. Here and there along the columns rifle shots sounded out as the soldiers fired into the air to see if their powder was still dry.

General Hood was cheered by his men as he rode along the marching lines. Here was Hood, who had saved the army from Atlanta, had given them health and self-confidence again, and had promised that Thomas's army would be destroyed. The very look of him was the look of hope.

John Bell Hood was born in Kentucky but claimed Texas as his home. At the battle of Gettysburg, Hood received a wound in the left arm, permanently depriving him the use of it. He led several divisions through General Wood's gap in the Union lines at the battle of Chickamauga, where he received a wound in his right leg, requiring amputation of it a mere four and one-half inches from his body. Such wounds would have caused many men to quit, but Hood returned to duty, disregarding the fact that he was so crippled that he had to be strapped into the saddle so that he might ride or sit. He admired President Davis so much that he had named his mount "Jeff Davis."

Hood knew that Sherman's army was marching south, but if he could entice Sherman back to Tennessee, he could save the Confederacy. If Sherman did not return to give battle in Tennessee as Hood wanted, then the Confederate army would defeat Thomas, march on into Kentucky, cross the mountains, and join Lee for a decisive blow against Grant! It was a desperate and dramatic project, but Hood was capable of such a feat.

The Army of Tennessee was organized into three fine infantry corps, commanded by Gens. Benjamin F. Cheatham, Alexander P. Stewart, and Stephen D. Lee.

Benjamin F. Cheatham was the oldest corps commander in Hood's army. A native Tennessean, he had served as a colonel of Tennessee infantry during the Mexican War. When Tennessee seceded and joined the Confederacy, Cheatham was made brigadier general in the Confederate army and soon was promoted to the rank of major general in March, 1862. He had served with the Army of Tennessee through all its battles since Shiloh. Cheatham was given a corps to command when Gen. William Hardee was transferred after the battle of Atlanta. Cheatham was highly regarded and had the reputation of being a hard fighter among the men who served under him.

Alexander P. Stewart was born in Rogersville, Tennessee, in 1821. Graduated from West Point in 1842, he resigned from the army in 1845 to teach mathematics and philosophy at Cumberland and Nashville universities in Tennessee. He was a Whig and had opposed secession. After Tennessee seceded, he joined the Confederate army. He soon became a major and fought at the battle of Belmont. At the battle of Shiloh, he was a brigadier general.

At Shiloh he received a head wound. His luck at that time had been extraordinary. A rifle ball had struck his hatband squarely and had broken the outer coating of his skull, but it failed to penetrate further because of the thicknesses of paper placed under the sweatband by him prior to the battle.

Stewart spent several weeks in Corinth, Mississippi, recovering from his wound. At the battle of Stone's River his brigade was ordered to make an assault. Stewart did not believe that the attack could succeed but went forward as ordered with his men. After a furious fight his brigade was forced back woefully with a forty-three percent loss.

In June, 1863, he was promoted to major general, commanding a division in Hardee's corps. During the Atlanta campaign, he became lieutenant general and took over a corps. He was a man of strong character and competent military ability. His men nicknamed him "Old Straight."

Stephen D. Lee was born in Charleston, South Carolina, in 1833. He was graduated from West Point in 1854 and served in Florida. Lee rose rapidly in the Confederate ranks, beginning with Fort Sumter. In 1862 he was with the Army of Northern Virginia, mainly with artillery commands. Promoted to brigadier general, Lee fought at Vicksburg and was named major general. In June, 1864, he was made a lieutenant general, the youngest in the Confederacy. He fought well at Tupelo and Atlanta. As an officer, he proved very capable and often heroic.

Each corps consisted of three divisions. Of the nine divisions, there was one whose divisional commander was showing potential corps command. His name was Patrick R. Cleburne.

General Patrick R. Cleburne was born in County Cork, Ireland. He had served in the British army and came to the United States in 1849, settling in Helena, Arkansas, as a druggist. In 1856 he became a lawyer, but in 1860 he organized the Yell Rifles, a local home-guard unit. Upon secession of Arkansas, Cleburne was made a captain and later colonel of the infantry. By early 1862 he was a major general and distinguished himself in fighting at Murfreesboro, Chickamauga, and in repulsing Sherman at Missionary Ridge. Cleburne urged that slaves be freed and used in the army, an opinion that may have kept him from commanding a corps. Cleburne was known as the "Stonewall Jackson of the West," so strongly did he hold the affection and respect of his men.

Hood marched his three corps of twenty-nine brigades (with over 150 guns) and miles of wagons northward. Alexander P. Stewart headed for Lawrenceburg, Benjamin F. Cheatham's corps headed toward Waynesboro, while Stephen D. Lee's corps, mainly using back-country roads to keep out of sight of prying Yankees, moved toward a point between the two towns. The rebels were feeling good and felt that this time they were headed for victory. In Georgia they had been on the defensive, for which they were not suited. Now they were on the offensive, with their faces grim and set for Union blood.

Hatch and Croxton prudently fell back before Hood's army, so thin and ragged in actual appearance, so greatly magnified by rumor and fear. General Croxton withdrew toward Pulaski; Hatch, in order to protect Schofield's flank, fell back to Lawrenceburg. The divisions of Buford and Jackson got across Shoal Creek without much trouble and began to advance upon Lawrenceburg from the west.

Hatch chose to remain in position and put up a fight. His men were armed with new-model carbines, Sharps single-shot breechloaders, which could be fired much faster than the muzzle-loading rifles the infantry had.

Buford pushed his skirmishers forward. Hatch's troopers opened up with a vicious volley, so vicious, in fact, that some of the weapons burst. The rebels withdrew but came thundering up a side road and ran into a deadly fire from the Eleventh Indiana. The firing rose in sound as rebels and Yankees blazed away at less than a hundred yards.

General Bell's dismounted rebel brigade emerged from some woods with rifles and shotguns blazing. Bell's troops got within seventy yards and broke under the withering fire from Hatch's men. Another rebel battle line went forward, and the Northern and Southern boys got into a blind, flagitious fight with sabers. The Confederates finally were repulsed.

William Jackson brought up his artillery. When the Union troops noticed the guns about to go into action, they slowly withdrew through the timber, firing as they went.

Some of the withdrawing lines could be seen by the Confederate gunners, and the shells began to come over fast. Back into the outskirts of Lawrenceburg retreated the Union troopers.

Then there was a great rush and a pounding of hoofs as Jackson's artillery dashed into another firing line—three batteries coming up at a mad gallop, drivers lashing the

The Invasion

six-horse teams into firing line. The guns began to plaster Hatch's men again, and the air above them was filled with clods of dirt and flying, broken carbines as the shells ripped among them.

Hatch ordered retreat. It was becoming clear that the Union line could not be held with rebel guns hitting the line with paralyzing blows, and they were blowing shot and shell all over Lawrenceburg. The woods were full of Yankee fugitives looking desperately for the rear. From the south and west Jackson's men kept edging in closer, rolling their guns forward through the broken timber. Hatch's division fled toward Pulaski, with the exception of Horace Capron's brigade, which retreated toward Henryville.

There was a running fight between Capron and Rucker's rebel brigade from Lawrenceburg to Henryville. Just outside of Henryville, Capron turned to make a stand. Rucker, in close columns of squadrons, rode right over him and sent the Union troopers pell-mell through Henryville with rebels on their heels.

Outside of Mount Pleasant, Capron's bluecoats laid down withering carbine fire, but Rucker's men surged forward, swinging their sabers like madmen, and, again, Capron's men broke and fled to Columbia.

Hatch, with the rest of his division, was pursued so hard by Forrest's men that he was forced to turn and move toward the village of Campbellsville. There was a fight all the way into the village and even a good, brisk street fight, with stray shots from carbines hitting houses.

A column of rebel horsemen approached from the north. Again, Hatch turned, heading back toward Pulaski. Over the muddy fields rode Hatch's men with a swarm of yelling, firing rebels on their heels.

Schofield received word that Hatch, under heavy fire, had withdrawn from Lawrenceburg. Schofield knew if rebels were at Lawrenceburg, then he was in a bad spot. Schofield sent word to General Thomas, informing him about Hatch and that he felt Pulaski should be given up to the rebels.

Thomas realized that Schofield was being outflanked and ordered him to withdraw from Pulaski to Columbia, set up new positions, and hold Hood from there.

Schofield began to pull back his 22,000 men and trains as soon as he received orders to do so. In a dismal rain, through hub-deep muddy roads with their heavy loads, men and animals pushed slowly toward Columbia.

The columns were in such a hurry to get to Columbia that surplus baggage and camp equipment were left by the roadside, and the men, with their uniforms encased in mud, plodded on with their heads down.

Forrest's cavalry was driving in hard from the southwest. Short, fierce firefights raged along the Union columns. It fell to the lot of General Croxton to cover the retreat.

Chapter III

Pulaski to Spring Hill

Several miles from Pulaski, General Croxton saw that, if he could get a unit up on a little rise of ground, the rebels might be held back. So he sent the Eighth Tennessee (Union) and Sixty-fifth Indiana infantry off to tend to it.

The two regiments went forward cautiously, since Chalmer's rebel troopers were crack shots. When the regiments began to draw fire from three directions, they went storming up the hill, firing as they went. Struggling through dense thickets that seemed to be alive and humming with bullets, they forced the rebels to give way.

The regiments took defensive positions to await the expected countercharge. Behind them Schofield's army moved like a slow snake toward Columbia. The sun had broke through the clouds, promising a pleasant day, and the men smiled because they were tired of rain. The rebel Forrest pushed skirmishers forward, and there was a bit of long-range artillery, but for the most part the Confederates seem content to let the two regiments remain where they were.

Schofield's army continued on to Columbia without further serious harassment. As they neared Columbia they could hear rumble of gunfire where Cox and the advance forces were holding off Rucker's cavalry.

Amid cheers, Schofield and his staff cantered up to a hilltop overlooking the valley beyond, with steeples and housetops of a town showing in the distance. The town that

SPRING HILL
APPROX. 4:30 P.M.

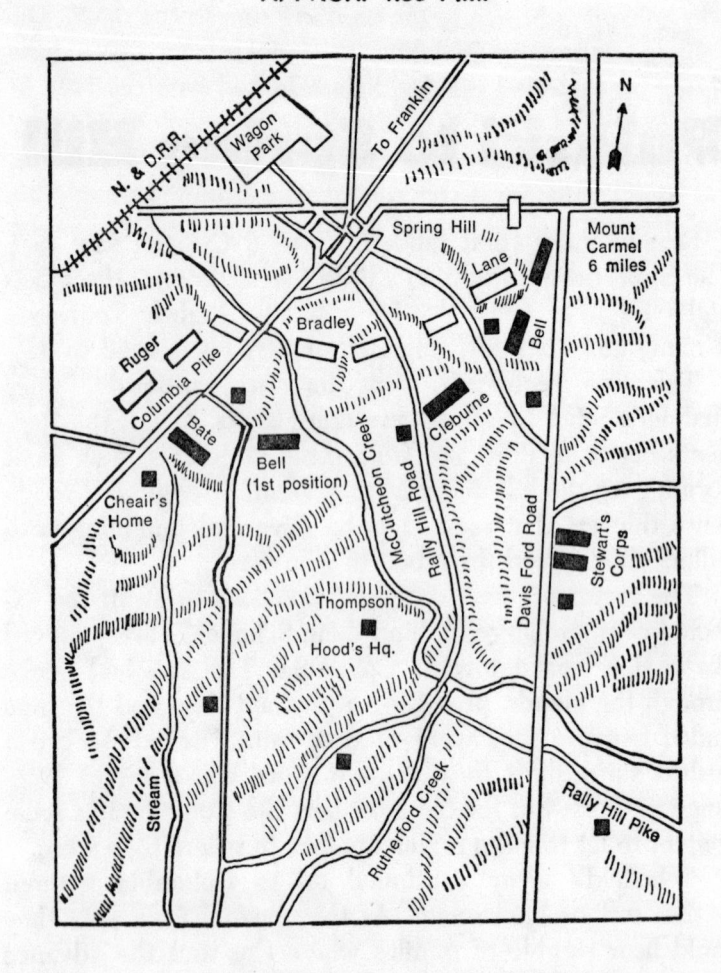

he could see beyond the hills was Columbia, with the Duck River, gleaming brown in the morning sun, to the north. Off to the southwest he could see the smoke from Cox's guns holding off the rebel cavalry. Schofield had won the race to Columbia.

On the afternoon of November 25, Hood was standing atop a hill examining the rolling countryside through his field glasses. Flags, guns, and moving troops were to be seen on the slopes south of Columbia. Schofield's army had stopped retreating and had turned to fight.

Hood deployed Stewart's corps around Schofield. Sporadic cannon fire and light skirmishing were waging, but Hood made no effort to attack in force. He spent the rest of the afternoon in violent artillery exchanges while he tried to decide where he could cross the Duck to flank Schofield out of his lines.

On the morning of the Twenty-sixth, Schofield received orders from Thomas to hold the north side of the Duck River, keeping Hood south of the river until ample forces could be gathered at Nashville to cope with the Army of Tennessee.

In the rain that afternoon Schofield moved the bulk of his trains to the north bank using the railroad bridge. Schofield intended to bring his infantry over after dark but the all-day rain rendered the approach to the bridge impassable, so the infantry crossing was postponed.

By morning of the Twenty-seventh, the nine divisions of the Army of Tennessee had deployed in front of Columbia with the right lapping over the Mount Pleasant and Pulaski pikes. Near Hood's headquarters at Ashwood Hall, the home of Col. Andrew Polk, Cheatham placed his corps between the two pikes, and Stewart's corps camped along the Mount Pleasant pike, with its rear elements about two miles north of Mount Pleasant.

General Patrick Cleburne noticed the beauty of St. John's Church in its quiet grove on the road to Ashwood. "If I should happen to die in battle," he said to his aide, "I should like nothing better than to be buried there; it is almost worth dying to be buried in such a spot."

Schofield finished moving his infantry across the Duck, setting up stronger positions than the ones he left. The Union trenches zigzagged along the lower slopes of the hills, anchored at proper intervals with built-up redoubts facing the river. It appeared to Hood that no imaginable frontal assault could carry their positions. Also, it was beginning to rain again. A late November rain is apt to be a long one, and the Duck is capable of rising six feet in twenty-four hours when the rain comes down. General Hood did not want to give battle with a deep river behind him. So, instead of the great drama of a cannonade and a mighty assault by storming battle lines, Hood dug in to decide his next move.

The two armies lay close together here with nothing between them but the Duck River. Both sides lined their cannon and dug more trenches. Many Confederate and Union soldiers lay down behind trees and underbrush and began blazing away across the stream. This resulted in killing a few dozen boys but decided nothing about the outcome of the campaign.

Hood, for once in his military career, came up with a fairly good plan. He would cross the Duck beyond Schofield's flank, make a sweeping movement to Spring Hill, twelve miles north of Columbia. With Spring Hill in rebel hands, Schofield's troops, which made up the largest part of General Thomas's forces, would be stopped, surrounded, and captured.

General Stephen D. Lee's corps, with virtually all of Hood's artillery, would be left on the south side to keep

Schofield's attention until the rest of the army could cross the river to Schofield's rear.

On the morning of November 28, Forrest's cavalry, at a gallop and with flashing sabers, splashed across the Duck River at Huey's Mill, eight miles above Columbia. Hood was to follow the cavalry with the corps of Stewart and Cheatham. If Hood could beat Schofield to Spring Hill, his boast of a "Stonewall Jackson Movement" would be good.

After crossing the river, Forrest encountered Wilson's cavalry. All afternoon the woods north of the Duck River trembled with rolling gunfire. Here and there in the woods, Wilson's regiments tried to make a stand, but Forrest's men beat them down and swept over them. Back northeast past Rally Hill and Hurt's Corners toward Triune, east of Franklin, Wilson's hard-pressed cavalry was forced back under a hail of bullets.

At dusk on the twenty-eighth of November, Hood, riding at the head of his heavy infantry columns, crossed the Duck. As the files crossed, huge fires were lit on each bank to help the men see where they were going. The flames attracted Union scouts, who reported to Schofield that the Confederate infantry was crossing.

Schofield, not yet sure what was happening, kept trying to get in touch with Wilson. He knew that Forrest was over on the north side, and, if rebel infantry was crossing in force, it was just possible that Hood might have the idea to swing around and hit the army's left, and Cox had sent a message earlier to Schofield suggesting that he consider the possibility of being flanked. Yet, the rebels were making a lot of racket in front of Columbia as if they intended to attack at any moment. Stay put or pull back? Schofield did not know which to do.

Around three o'clock in the morning, Schofield received a dispatch from Garrand of Wilson's cavalry advising him to:

"Get to Franklin without delay!" The dispatch sparked Schofield into action. He would pull the army back to Spring Hill, division by division. Schofield was still worried about the rebels in front of Columbia.

General Schofield started his wagon train toward Spring Hill early on the morning of November 29. As train guard, he assigned Wagner's division of Stanley's Fourth Army Corps. Schofield kept the rest of his army in line facing Lee's corps, while the bulk of the Confederate Army marched around his flank.

On the south bank of the Duck River, Lee had wheeled scores and scores of guns into line—ten- and twenty-pounder Parrotts, twelve-pounder Napoleons to bombard the Union trenches. His orders were simple: "Keep the Yankees' attention and make them think that the entire Confederate Army is getting ready to attack."

Before dawn on the Twenty-ninth, Lee's guns shook windows and made the ground quiver as he blasted Schofield's lines. The Union troops hugged the breastworks to escape the deadly explosions. The pounding was terrible. Caissons and limber chests were exploding, sending large fountains of black smoke into the air.

Schofield, squatting on his heels, was trying to observe the Confederate lines, but all he could see through the morning mist was a solid sheet of red flame from Lee's guns. About ten o'clock Schofield pulled Stanley's Fourth Corps out of the main line and sent them to join Wagner at Spring Hill.

Around noon, Bell's Confederate cavalry appeared before Spring Hill from the east. General Bell rode to a small rise, and in the distance he could see long lines of Yankee wagons moving slowly along the Columbia pike. Bell turned in his saddle and shouted a command. In a few minutes a rebel battery trotted forward and wheeled into firing position.

The rebel movement was observed by the alert Union officers. Colonel John Lane of Wagner's division, without waiting for orders, turned his brigade off the pike into line of battle facing east. They had hardly formed when Bell's four shells came screaming over, exploding in some woods to Lane's left.

Lane sent the Fifty-seventh Indiana forward from the protecting road bank to make the rebel battery withdraw. The Fifty-seventh charged through bushes, and the bang-bang of small-arms fire from dismounted Confederate troopers began to drop some of the Indiana boys. The regiment stopped and fired one volley, pulling back with the second volley.

Wagner rushed the Seventy-third Illinois into Spring Hill and none too soon. Abraham Buford's rebel cavalry, coming up the Rally Hill pike, was headed directly for Spring Hill. Outside of town the rebels and Yankees clashed. The Seventy-third deployed two companies as skirmishers; the rest of the regiment quickly threw up fence rails for protection. Toward the rails rushed Buford's men, and the Seventy-third fired an effective volley that sent Buford's men diving for cover. The rebels reformed and drove in again, but the Seventy-third put in a smashing volley that sent Buford's bleeding men reeling back.

On the right there was a rough fight as Lane's men, at close range, repulsed a Confederate charge. The men in gray charged out of the woods, dashing toward Lane's position. Lane's men received them in long, echoing volleys, causing the Confederates to retreat.

Crossing Rutherford Creek was more Confederate cavalry. These fresh troopers joined Bell, and, at about three o'clock that afternoon, the first serious assault against the Union lines by Confederate cavalry was made. Forrest's men forced their way through thickets and over ravines, firing as they came with clouds of dust over them. Volleys ripped at them; men and horses toppled, but Forrest's troopers pressed on until a Yankee battery blew away the head of the charge with canister.

General Stanley had finished parking Schofield's eight hundred wagons on the pike between the town and railroad station, placing Opdycke's brigade on the north across the pike, protecting the wagons and artillery. Stanley shifted Lane from his first position to the east and southeast. Bradley's command was bought forward to support Lane.

The lull ended at four o'clock when a line of rebels rose from the slopes in front of Lane's men and began to give the Yankees a heavy fire. Then, from the woods beyond, a heavy battle line of Confederate infantry emerged, coming up the slope with their red-and-blue battle flags snapping in the breeze, Pat Cleburne's men, yelling and eager for combat.

Cleburne's troops had formed in line of battle, after crossing Davis Ford, off the Rally Hill road about three o'clock, with General Hood personally planning and directing the action. Cleburne's men waited while the Confederate cavalry fought. Word came at around four that the Yankees had given the cavalry rough handling and would win the battle unless somebody did something about it. So the Texans, Tennesseans, and Mississippians stormed out to do something about it.

Cleburne's troops struck Bradley's line, and a long, tearing crackle of rifle fire broke over the meadows. The Forty-fifth Alabama, with the Eighth Mississippi, found cover around some farmhouses and began to give the Twenty-sixth Ohio a bad time. It was a strange fight for a while—a stand-up, straightaway battle with no advancing or retreating. Lane's men burned the slopes with rifle fire but had to give way before Cleburne's hard-driving men.

The Union forces retreated toward Spring Hill with Cleburne's men following them with jeering shouts. Two brigades from Forrest's command came in from below Spring Hill to add their weight to the pursuit. In the outskirts of town the flight was checked. General Stanley had brought up eighteen guns, placing them south of town across the pike. The guns became a strong point where the beaten Union soldiers could make a stand again.

The rebels were advancing on both sides of the pike, converging on the batteries, firing as they came. The guns fired double-shotted rounds of canister at the range of fifty feet, while the Union infantry fired volleys of musket bullets into the faces of Cleburne's men. The rebel column was smashed and the survivors withdrew sullenly. Cleburne's boys reformed quickly and went streaming again for the guns. Again the guns raked Cleburne's battle lines with heavy salvos. The rebels in front crumbled, the rest of the line simply melted away under the shells, and the men who were not hit ran back into fields out of range. General Bradley was badly wounded and lost one hundred and fifty men. Cleburne's attack had cost Hood five hundred men. Cleburne reformed his men for another assault but received orders to engage in no further action that night.

Cleburne pulled his men well to the south before halting for the night. Granbury's brigade, in the lead, formed along the Columbia pike facing northwest, with Lowrey's brigade on its left and more to the south, and Govan's Arkansas brigade to the left of Lowrey's. General Cleburne established division headquarters in a farmer's yard east of the turnpike, and his troops spread their blankets on the ground and turned in for some sleep.

About five o'clock, General Bate's division arrived on the field. Hood directed him to form a battle line north of the Cheairs' home. General Jackson's brigade formed first and began to advance with his Georgia troops. The Georgians had moved only about two hundred yards when the Twenty-sixth Ohio of Lane's brigade began to blister their lines with rifle fire. The Yankees were behind a stone wall, and it seemed to blaze from end to end with one crackling sheet of red flame. Up came a second brigade, swinging across the road and rolling forward into the battle smoke to help Jackson. The stone wall blazed out again but the Confederates pushed on hard. The Ohio men left the stone wall and began pulling back toward Spring Hill still sending lead into Bate's troops.

Bate thrust on with bullets knocking his men left and right. Suddenly, the Confederates realized that something had gone very wrong. Great, rolling volleys of rifle fire were coming in behind the Confederates. The rebel regiments wheeled around in time to catch the onslaught of General Ruger's division, which was the head of Schofield's army coming from Columbia.

Bate gave Ruger every bullet he had, but the Union boys kept coming on with flags flying. A savage Yankee charge came in from the right, and the Sixty-sixth Georgia took it head-on, exchanging volleys at a bare ten yards. General Bate hurried back to his third brigade, trying to get a couple of regiments wheeled for flank protection. But Bate's support of a Confederate battery was ready and waiting. The battery commander held his men in until the Union troops were within point-blank range, and then with canister salvos the Union charge was broken.

Bate's brigades advanced again with a grim determination that would have taken them through Schofield's entire army, but before they came under fire, orders arrived from Cheatham directing them to shift position to their right and form on Cleburne's left to confront Bradley and Lane.

The Confederate high command was disturbed about the

rough handling Cleburne had received and wanted more troops to beat down Bradley and Lane. For some odd reason the racket created by Ruger's attack had not carried far. Hood, not knowing that Bate was engaged with Schofield's main force, had ordered Cheatham to bring Bate to Cleburne's support. When Bate's brigades began to form on Cleburne's left, they were shocked to find Cleburne's men camped for the night instead of preparing for battle.

Brown's rebel division began to arrive on Cleburne's right. This division was ordered by Cheatham to attack. Brown went to work forming his lines, but he was surprised to learn that he had no support on his flank. His support was cooking supper, he was told. Brown sent a courier to Cheatham explaining his plight. Yet, mindful of his orders until they were rescinded, he began banging away with two guns and made a prodigious racket. Brown soon received new orders not to attack but to dig in at his present position. By seven o'clock the firing had completely ceased, and most of the Confederate regiments stacked arms and began to eat supper sitting on their knapsacks.

General A. P. Stewart's corps advanced up Davis Ford road south of Rutherford Creek about two and one-half miles south of Spring Hill. As his troops tramped along, they heard the heavy firing from Cleburne's assault and later, to their left, the throbbing of Bate's guns in the northeast. Stewart's men quickened their pace expecting action, but they veered away from the sound of firing, heading directly north. Stewart was trying to place his corps to the right of Spring Hill to box in the Union forces.

But Stewart did not get his corps north of Spring Hill. On the march, he received orders to retrace his route and to form on Cheatham's flank. It was pitch-dark, and Stewart's corps, after turning around, was unable to get their proper bearings on the winding, back-country roads. Finally, around midnight, his men went into bivouac without ever finding Cheatham's right flank.

Major General Ed Johnson's division of Lee's corps arrived on the field about ten o'clock in the evening. After forming his battle lines in the dark, Johnson sent his brigades stumbling across the broken ground. As the rebels advanced, they smelled acrid smoke and began to fall over bodies and shattered limbs of trees lying on the ground in a tangle. The lines halted while Johnson tried to find out just where his division was. Unable to locate his position on the maps and receiving no further orders, Johnson had his men pitch camp on the ground where Bate had fought earlier.

The Confederate and Union armies were mixed up by the scattered marching and fighting. The Columbia pike was jammed with men from both sides. One Confederate squadron fell in beside a wagon train only to discover that the wagoners were wearing blue instead of gray. Someone fired his rifle, other shots were fired, and men struck blindly at one another in the dark. The rebel troopers broke off the fight, riding off into the darkness.

On the Columbia pike there was a yelling, confused, stumbling mass of men and horses. Here and there in the woods, regiments and parts of regiments from both sides were blundering into one another. Flashes of gunfire ripped the night air. Hood's grand plan for a "Stonewall Jackson Movement" had ended in a state of mass confusion.

William Jackson's mounted rebels were attempting to cut the highway at Thompson Station. At a mad gallop his troops thundered down the dark road, crashing squarely into the middle of a Yankee regiment. There was a wild, confused melee with nobody knowing what was happening, Confederates as surprised as Federals, and troopers slashing with sabers and taking bullets in return. A good many of Jackson's men were shot from their horses. The Confederates finally withdrew, their mission unaccomplished.

Schofield's army was pushing along the Columbia pike; there were rebels all around, but none across the Columbia pike itself. Everyone was confused except Schofield; he kept urging his staff to get their brigades through before the rebels could collect their senses.

General Hood was told by some of his officers that the Union army was getting away. Hood turned to Forrest—could he block the road with his cavalry? Forrest replied that his troops were without ammunition.

Hood was stumped. His ammunition trains were in the rear, with Lee back at Columbia. General Jackson walked in and, upon hearing of Hood's plight, told them that his men had captured some ammunition a few hours before. Forrest jumped up, saying that he would take it and do his best to block the pike.

At three o'clock in the morning the Union trains were attacked at Thompson Station, and ten wagons were burned by Forrest's hard-riding troopers before they were driven off by sleepy Union soldiers. The pike remained open, and the last of Schofield's wagons creaked north out of Spring Hill about daylight.

When morning came, the Confederates had Spring Hill to themselves with nothing but dead men lying around. Schofield had slipped his entire army through the rebels and was safely on his way to Franklin.

General Hood and his generals sat down for breakfast at the home of Maj. Nat Cheairs outside of Spring Hill. Before they finished eating, bitter and hot words flew. Hood accused Cheatham and Cleburne of allowing Schofield to escape the trap. Swords flashed as the generals demanded apologies. Hood, in a rage, stormed out of the house still thinking that he had planned a masterpiece military move and his staff had failed him.

Masterpiece military move? It was, rather, a dreary series of missed opportunities—a commanding general's dream to net an entire army. But not once had the commanding general put out his hand to pull his plan together and to undo his own mistakes. The plan had been left to work by itself, and the general was a spectator; and in the end it had been a failure by the smallest of margins. General Hood had no one to blame for the failure but himself.

The Army of Tennessee broke camp to resume the pursuit. Confederate anger was in the air. Schofield had evaded them at Pulaski, Columbia, and now Spring Hill. There was still a chance to catch Schofield at Franklin and destroy him, and the Army of Tennessee, with its battle blood up, intended to do just that. Toward Franklin the grumbling, bitter troops streamed to reap their wrath upon Schofield.

Chapter IV

Franklin

The town of Franklin is bounded on the east and north sides by the Harpeth River, which makes a right-angled bend in its general course, the town lying within the angle at the edge of a gentle plateau which rises from the water's edge on a hill on the north bank of the river.

Near the Nashville and Decatur railroad bridge was Fort Granger, a dismantled earthwork built two years before by other Union forces when they were at Franklin. The guns in the fort well commanded the railroad bridge and a deep cut in the railway near the point where it touches the river not far from the Lewisburg pike.

General Schofield, arriving in Franklin on the morning of November 30, became upset upon learning that the pontoons he had ordered had not arrived. The clumsy wooden scows with which the army built its pontoon bridges were miles away from where Schofield's army was waiting. The weary engineers, wrestling personally with the ungainly things, had no idea that anybody in particular wanted them or that there was any special hurry about anything.

No pontoons, no bridges; no bridges, no crossing of the river. Schofield, in order to get his army across someway, turned the command over to Gen. Jacob D. Cox so he could devote his energy to improving the fords and repairing the bridges.

The Union line of works, about two miles long, extended

BATTLE ARRAY AT FRANKLIN

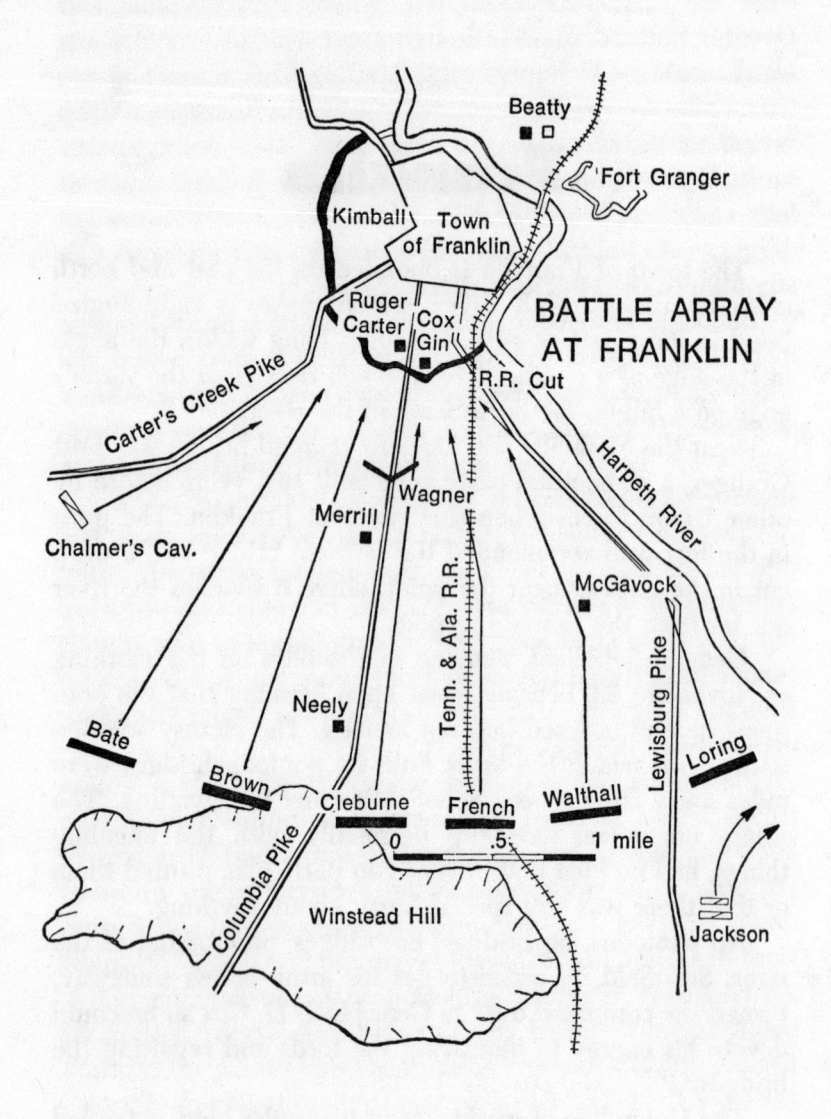

from the extreme Federal left, where the Nashville and Decatur railroad passed through a cut near the river, westward across the Columbia pike, bending back across Carter's Creek pike west of the town, with outworks following a deep ravine to the river on the other side. Two miles further south of the Union line was a comparatively high range of hills known as Winstead Hill, where Wagner's division was digging pits for the guns and banking earth up expecting any minute the vanguard of Hood's army.

Schofield's engineers found the piles of a burned bridge in position, sawed them down an inch or two where the water had quenched the flames, and laid a crude corduroy of planks; in the afternoon Schofield's wagons and artillery, in slow file, began to cross the makeshift bridge with water sloshing round the horses' hocks.

Back on Winstead Hill, Wagner's division had just finished its digging in when the vanguard of Hood's army appeared off in the distance. Wagner had only two brigades, but they were good ones. One was composed of four Illinois regiments and two regiments from Ohio, led by Col. Joseph Conrad. Wagner's other fine brigade was under the command of Col. John Q. Lane.

Stewart's column halted when the rebels saw Union troops ahead of them. Stewart was a trained soldier who knew the folly of smashing head-on into a perfect defensive position; so he decided to swing a couple of his divisions down Henpeck Lane to outflank Wagner. The shock divisions of Loring and Walthall began moving down the lane.

To divert Wagner's attention from the flanking movement, Stewart pushed the Twenty-ninth North Carolina of Ector's brigade forward as skirmishers. Coming up through the woods, the Tarheels caught it from a slim Union skirmish line hidden behind trees. The Yankees here were good marksmen, and woods fighting was their specialty. They went dodging back from tree to tree, reloading under cover and drawing a good aim before they fired. But the Carolina troops came from mountain country and were pretty good riflemen themselves. The rebels cleared the woods at last, and Wagner had gotten glimpses of a big rebel infantry column trudging through the woods heading east. Wagner was no Napoleon, but he knew that he was being outflanked and ordered his division to pull back.

Wagner's two brigades moved quickly down the pike and halted on a little rise about half a mile in advance of the main Union line. Wagner sent a note to headquarters requesting permission to remain in his advanced position. His request was granted, but if Hood made an advance in force, he was to pull back to the main line.

Stewart's two divisions emerged onto the Lewisburg pike. Without waiting for further orders, they began to deploy into line of battle, with Loring's elite division on the extreme right and to his left the division of Walthall. Stewart placed French's division to Walthall's left.

As Stewart was forming his battle lines, General Hood, surrounded by his staff, their orderlies, the headquarters guard and all the rest, with headquarters flag flying, were on top of Winstead Hill examining the Union position. The reddish earthworks, with scores of guns bleak and silent in the sunlight, their muzzles staring blankly toward the Confederates, apparently made no impression upon Hood. He turned to his staff and told them to form their men for attack.

General Forrest bitterly opposed it contending that he could flank the Yankees from their works with the addition of one strong infantry division to his cavalry. Cheatham and Cleburne also expressed their opposition, but Hood was adamant and dramatically said, "We will make the fight," ordering Cheatham and Forrest to "drive the enemy from his position into the river at all hazards."

Cheatham turned and walked away to carry out his orders. He placed Cleburne's division to French's left and to the right of the Columbia pike with its left on the pike. To his left was Brown and then Bate on Brown's left. Lee's corps and most of Hood's artillery had not yet come up. Hood was going to attack even without proper artillery support for his infantry.

General Forrest, as directed, placed Jackson's division and Bell's brigade of Buford's cavalry on the right at McGavock Ford and Chalmer's division with Biffle and Dibrell on the extreme left.

Dust hung in the air as long columns of men, dressed in gray and tattered brown, crossed the highway and passed through woods, coming out on the lower side of Winstead Hill, and began to align along the Widow Neely's farmhouse, which was one-half mile north of Winstead Hill.

Guibor's Missouri battery of Stewart's corps, with gun carriages bouncing wildly with spinning wheels, swung off into the fields and sent six polished guns into line to the tune of high-sounding bugle calls on the Confederate right. Captain Presstman pulled his six guns to the top of Merrill Hill. In a few minutes his battery was lined up on the slope, limbers a dozen yards to the rear, men taking horses back, and gun crews busy with ramrod and handspike to support the Confederate left.

Wagner observed the movements and sent word back to Schofield that the rebels were ranking as if they were getting ready to attack.

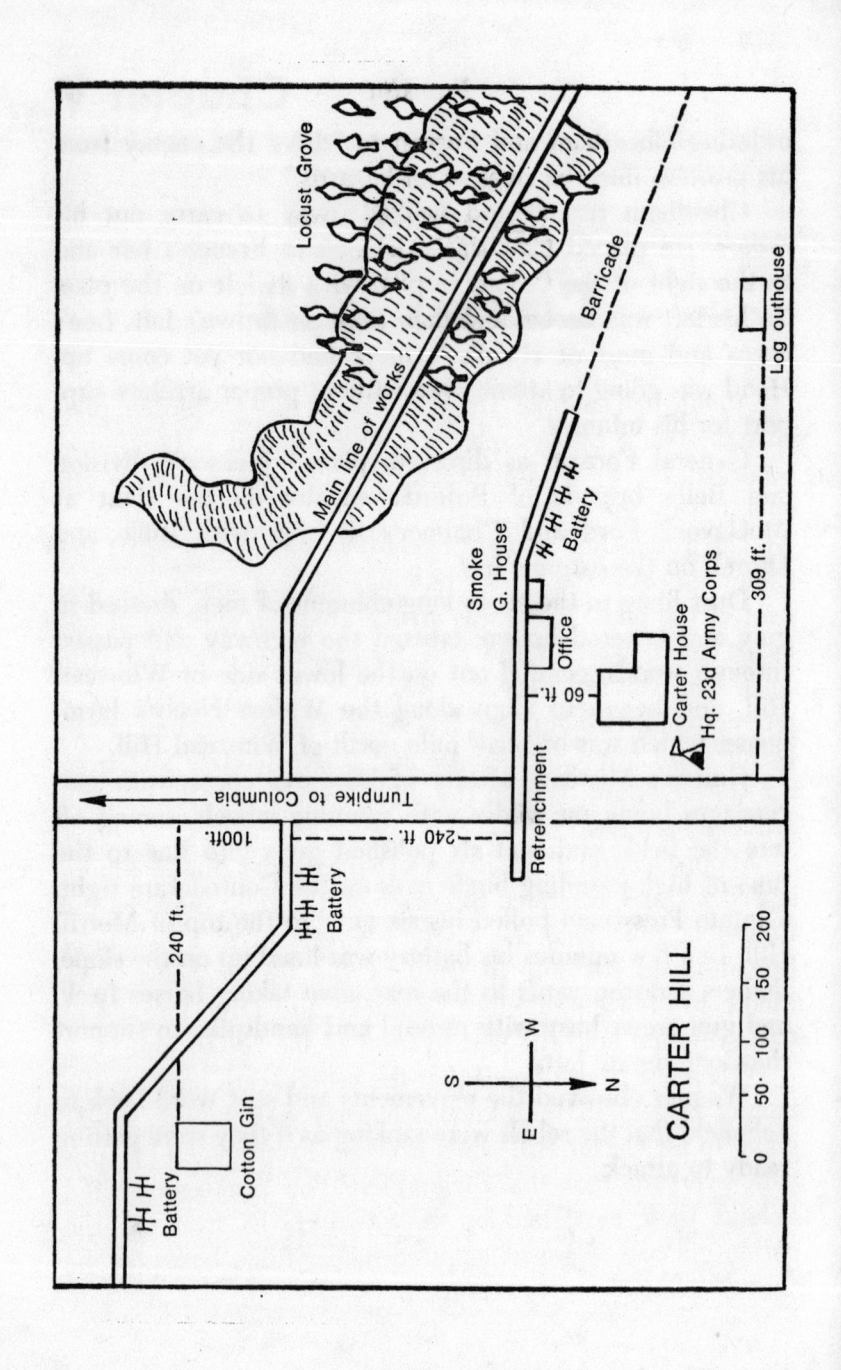

CARTER HILL

Locust Grove

Main line of works

Barricade

Smoke G. House

Office

Battery

Carter House
Hq. 23d Army Corps

Log outhouse

309 ft.

60 ft.

Retrenchment

Turnpike to Columbia →

240 ft.

100 ft.

Battery

240 ft.

Battery

Cotton Gin

0 50 100 150 200

N S E W

Chapter V

Carter Hill

About half a mile from Franklin the Columbia pike passed over a hill, near which was situated a farmhouse occupied by F. B. Carter and family and a cotton gin operated by the Carter family.

The Union line was strongest here where it crossed the Columbia pike, the Carter house being just inside the line west of the pike. There was a rude abatis, consisting of cut locust trees, west of the pike just south of the line. The main line was open at the pike but was protected by a retrenchment two hundred feet back. This retrenchment ran beside the Carter smokehouse and was only sixty feet from the Carter house. Within the area, there were three Union artillery batteries.

Major General T. H. Ruger's two brigades, under Moore and Strickland, occupied the space on the right between the Columbia pike and the Carter's Creek pike. Strickland's brigade held the line in front of the Carter house with Moore to his right. Reilly's Kentucky and Ohio brigade of Cox's division held the part in front of the cotton gin.

When the troops heard that the rebels were ranking, the men of Ruger's division knew whatever was coming, it was going to hit Carter Hill when it came. From general to private, everyone took that for granted. The Yankees cowered behind their earth-and-log breastworks. In front of the cotton gin one regiment emptied its cartridge boxes on the logs in front for easier access in reloading. Cox walked along the line, checking to see that the guns were ready and that the ammunition chests were full.

About four o'clock six shells from Guibor's battery screamed over the Union line. There was a quick ripple of movement all along the Yankee line as thousands of men sprang to their feet and ran to their places.

Hood's twelve guns roared, shooting out quick jets of red flame and rolling clouds of blackish white smoke, breaking the air with heavy sound. At the time, General Hood ordered his infantry to advance!

The Union soldiers looked out across the fields, and their hearts began to beat faster. Up and down the Union firing line ran a low murmur: "There they are . . . here comes the infantry!"

Rank after rank came out to march across a two-mile-wide valley to the low hill where the Union troops were waiting with shotted guns. The sight was majestic: fighting soldiers lined up from flank to flank, slashed red flags overhead, sunlight flashing upon their bayonets, lines dressed as if for parade.

Pat Cleburne's famous division, composed of men from Arkansas, Alabama, Mississippi, Tennessee, and Texas, was headed straight for Carter Hill. Cleburne's division was a typical Cheatham unit—good marchers, outstanding on offense, able to stand up under heavy casualties and produce tremendous firepower. Cleburne was a dedicated Confederate, and he kept fine control of his brigades.

To Cleburne's right was the division of Maj. Gen. John C. Brown. His four brigades were hard-hitting and under excellent brigadier generals. Brown massed his men for greater impact, Gordon and Gist in front with Carter and Strahl in close support.

Long and bright and perfectly aligned, the lines crossed

the fields. No rebel yell now, the men were coming on silently, carrying their rifles, with fixed bayonets, at right shoulder arms. The firing and the yelling would come later.

Wagner's line, in its exposed position, was out in front of the army. Its left and right had no support. With the rebels moving in fast, Wagner saw it was too late to withdraw—he would have to stay where he was and make the best of it. He rode along the line telling the men to be calm and not to fire until the rebels got in close, and the gray lines came swinging up the slopes, nearer and nearer.

Conrad's brigade would get it first, and the rebels moved in on him. Conrad's men poured out a fire that took a frightful toll, and the Union artillery tore ragged holes in the neat ranks, and for the moment Cleburne's assault was beaten back.

On Wagner's right there were rolling smoke clouds and a tremendous racket of firing and yelling men. Lane's men fired point-black into the faces of Brown's troops, but the rebels here were in one large mass. John Brown was throwing his men in remorsefully and they were great fighters. Men fought by regiments and by companies. The wild uproar of battle rose as Cleburne's troops rolled forward against Conrad again.

Something had to give, and the break came first where Lane was. The rebels were pouring in from three sides, laying down a killing fire, and the brigade was dissolving in fire and smoke. With Lane giving way, Conrad's troops began to give ground, with Southern infantry firing fast from a ravine on one side, a new battle line charging in on the other. It was too much; Wagner's entire division broke and ran!

From Carter Hill, the Yankees in their works looked at a wild panorama of retreat. Thick battle smoke lay on the fields, and out of it came the swaying lines of Wagner's men, turning now and then to fire a volley at the gray masses right behind them. There was a maddening chaos in the fields: retreating regiments colliding with one another, rebel units intermingled with Yankees, and many Union soldiers running behind the rebel battle lines.

The men defending the main line had to open fire before all of Wagner's men could reach safety, so close were the rebels. Yelling Confederates came charging through the line, and a solid rebel brigade went plunging straight ahead for the Carter house. Men began to swing their rifles as clubs, everybody yelling and cursing, officers firing pistols, dense smoke settling down on everything. The Yankee line staggered back, and Carter Hill rang with rifle fire. Strahl's Tennessee brigade ran around the Carter house to finish things and ran smack into Opdycke's Illinois, Ohio, and Wisconsin brigade.

Opdycke's brigade had been placed north of the Carter house as reserve. When the terrible uproar of battle came closer and closer, he knew that the main line was being lost, so he swung his seven regiments into line just as the Tennesseans came charging in.

Carter Hill filled with smoke and flame and a great, ear-shattering noise as Opdycke's and Strahl's lines volleyed at point-blank range in blinding smoke. The men in and about the Carter buildings fired from the windows of the buildings and from every opening or interspace that could be used as a loophole.

The owner of the house, F. B. Carter, with two other men and nineteen women and children were in the cellar listening to the rain of bullets and shells against the house. In the rooms above them soldiers were running and firing. General Stanley ran up the stairs and fired pistols at the rebels from the upper window.

Outside, Strahl's men kept jamming in. The Tennesseans were not obeying their commands, although officers were shouting hoarsely and gesturing madly with their swords. No tactical move was possible in that jammed, smoky confusion, and no shouted command could be heard in the everlasting noise. It was just a mob of men trying to get in the middle of an enormous fight, rebel soldiers swarming in to get at their foes, all regimental formations lost, and every man going in on his own, swinging his rifle as a club.

It was hopeless odds; Opdycke's men kept pouring withering volleys into the Confederates. Strahl's men reeled back, leaving piles of flags, dead, and wounded in the Carter yard. The rebels halted in the ditch outside the earthworks and settled down among the logs for a sharp firefight.

Far behind the Union line Cox heard a new burst of shooting and yelling, which for as he knew that the other end of the line had caved in. Brigadier General George W. Gordon's Tennessee brigade had found a gap and was driving in from the southwest. Gordon pushed his troops on, with hand-to-hand fighting toward the Union rear. Fresh Union regiments led by Stanley closed in savagely on Gordon's men, getting them off balance and driving them back in wild rout. General Stanley went down with a bullet through his throat, but the Tennesseans were surrounded, and General Gordon, along with hundreds of his men, surrendered.

Near the cotton gin, Cleburne's troops charged home. One of his Mississippi regiments broke in among the guns and got into a wild, hand-to-hand fight with the cannoneers, who hit them with ramrods and handspikes. For a moment it seemed that this Mississippi regiment might break all the way through and get into Franklin. But the fire of the Union troops never stopped, and the Mississippians at last withdrew.

The Confederates would not give up; Cleburne drove his regiments against the Union line again. The breastworks blazed from end to end as the men from Indiana, Ohio, and Kentucky fired. The rebel line staggered, came to a halt, and began to drift slowly to its left.

Directly in front of the gin, Govan's Arkansas brigade had lagged behind the rest of the division's attack, but it kept its formation and headed for the line where Reilly's Yankee troops were. From the left, Lowrey's rebel regiments were running over to help, coming in through the smoke like a mob gone out of control.

There was not a mounted man to be seen. Cleburne's mount, "Red Pepper," had been killed earlier in the attack, and Cleburne was in the middle of the infantry, firing his pistol. A new fury of rifle fire hit the Confederates, and Pat Cleburne was killed while giving orders to his men. Some of the men from the Thirty-third Alabama picked him up, made a crude litter of muskets, and got him back to the rear.

Lowrey's Alabama and Mississippi brigades were dissolving under a heavy flank fire. In front they were getting canister that was too heavy to take, and there was no support in sight, but these rebels were tough and kept on going with Govan's men. The deadly, racking fire killed them by scores. The colonel of the Fifth Arkansas was shot as he tried to rally his regiment. The major took over and went down with bullets in his chest. The senior captain took over but was killed before he could give his first order. The colors were lost and the regiment fled along with the rest of Govan's and Lowrey's men.

Hiram Granbury, with sword in hand, led two regiments of his brigade toward the gin through the torrents of bullets, until a Union rifleman killed him, and what was left of the two regiments went streaming back into the smoky fields.

Carter Hill

Pat Cleburne's fine division was a wreck. His proud regiments had destroyed themselves in front of the cotton gin—*the* cotton gin, forever, after that bloody afternoon.

On the left, Gist's and Strahl's brigades stormed over the Union works again, exchanging deadly volleys at a scant fifteen yards. Slowly the Confederates were forced back to the breastworks. Once at the works, the rebels settled down and fired across the traverses. They refused to retreat from the works.

Brown's soldiers stood and fought over the traverses or around them with clubbed rifles and with bayonets. Bullets came in torrents. Where the graycoats were driven out a part of the trench, they took shelter in the outer ditch and threw bayoneted rifles over the parapet. Rebel and Yankee soldiers shot through the crevices and holes between the logs. The trench was filled with dead and wounded. An incessant fire was kept upon Brown's troops from front and flank. In all of the bloody fighting, there never had been such a struggle as this.

Brown's soldiers hung on in that horrible manner for hours and forced the Union troops to throw another barricade across the garden at the Carter house. Brown's losses were terrific; he himself was wounded. General Gist was slain. General Strahl, who just before the attack said, "Boys, this will be short, but desperate," was killed outright in the bloody, muddy ditch. General John C. Carter went down, mortally wounded, with five bullets in his body. Men less distinguished were no less conspicuous. Hundreds of enlisted men came willingly to the traverses to meet their death.

The divisions of Brown and Cleburne had lost nearly two thousand men killed and wounded—a fearful loss, considering that they had sent hardly seven thousand men into action.

The survivors formed a stomach-to-earth line of battle and maintained a feeble fire till about ten o'clock, when the exhausted troops were ordered to pull back. Brown's and Cleburne's staggering and wild-eyed troops, when they fell back, looked as if the fury of the fight around the earthworks, with only logs separating the combatants, had driven them mad.

Chapter VI

On the Right at Franklin

Major General William W. Loring was every inch a soldier, so much of a soldier he was to enter into foreign service to command the Egyptian Army after the war. General Loring was affable and extremely well liked by his troops.

Loring's division consisted of three fine brigades. He placed on his right the Mississippi brigade commanded by Brig. Gen. John Adams. In the center was Winfield S. Featherston's Mississippi brigade. General Scott found no room between Adams's left and Featherston's right and was ordered to deploy his Alabama and Louisiana brigade in the rear of Featherston's brigade in close support.

It was past four o'clock when Loring received word to go forward. Moving through woods and across gentle slopes, the men began to come under long-range artillery fire. The columns could be seen by the distant Union gunners and the shells were coming over fast. The rebels had hardly moved two hundred yards when one of the Yankee guns put a shell right in the middle of the Twenty-third Mississippi of Adams's brigade, killing several men.

As the lines cleared a deep ravine, they could see to their front broad fields, sloping gently up and down. Off to their right was an orchard, a patchwork of fences, and a large house, the home of a prosperous farmer named McGavock.

Into the hollow of the McGavock farm the gray lines marched under heavier fire, with wreaths of yellowish white smoke drifting above them. More men fell as Union cannon blasted the area around the McGavock farm, but the graycoats pushed on.

The width of the field contracted rapidly as Loring advanced, his front narrowing by the configuration of the ground and the course of the river. Also, his left flank was falling behind. Adams had to halt his brigade to await Featherston. Scott's brigade was nowhere in sight.

Featherston's panting men came up and then the two brigades pushed on. Soon Loring's infantry struck an unexpected obstacle in the railroad cut. The men were forced to change front and move by the left flank. As they wheeled, their flank was exposed to the guns at Fort Granger. The right regiments became enveloped in fire; whole companies went down as the shells ripped the cut.

The reserve brigade of Scott came up to plug the lines. Quickly, the remains of Adams's and Featherston's men reformed, and with Scott's troops they drove straight ahead through the Osage orange abatis. Moving through the abatis, Loring's troops were struck by ten Yankee guns from a hill directly to their front.

The breastworks were ahead with Union soldiers crouching low behind them. Colonel John S. Casement's brigade of Illinois and Indiana troops, armed with new breechloading repeating rifles, were waiting for the rebel lines to get close.

The Confederate lines halted, dressing its ranks under artillery fire. The waiting Yankee soldiers could hear the shouted commands of the rebel officers as the assaulting lines started forward. Up the slopes they came, four ranks deep, with bayonets flashing in the sunlight. With precision of step Loring's men moved, keeping time to the tap of deep-sounding drums.

At a shouted command, Casement's men leveled their rifles and fired, and a long sheet of flame ran from end to end of the barricade, and the Confederate charge ceased to look like a parade. The rebels halted, tried to reform, and the Union troops stood up and whacked in another volley. The Confederates went down in rows, dozens at a time. The Yankees whipped in another volley! Loring's troops got off an unsteady volley; a few rebels stumbled forward a few steps but were cut down by the hail of bullets. Loring's division fell apart. Some Confederates ran back to find shelter amid the deep bank of the railroad; others lay down on the ground among the dead and wounded to escape the deadly fire from Casement's brigade.

Loring rallied and reformed his brigades and in a few minutes they advanced again. The Yankee gunners, with canister and shell, knocked great holes in the gray ranks, and the earthworks blazed out as wickedly as ever. General Adams was riddled as his horse leaped the works. His mount fell dead with forefeet over the palisade. The few stalwart men who managed to climb the works were slain at point-blank range. Loring's decimated regiments were blown back by the torrential rifle fire.

But men still tried to storm the deadly works. General Thomas Scott rallied the Twenty-seventh and Fifty-fifth Alabama and led them in a new charge—taking a rifle himself to lead them in person. Across the railroad the Confederates went with the spine-chilling rebel yell.

The front of the rebel column was blown away. Then Brig. Gen. Thomas Scott fell seriously wounded from a minié ball. The Alabama boys withdrew to the railroad bank minus half of their numbers. Some waved their hands in the air, but through the dense smoke no one could see them trying to surrender, and they were shot down. Loring's dead lay in heaps near the railroad cut. Entire regiments had been mowed down by the repeating rifles. Loring's division was out of the fight.

Major General Edward C. Walthall, at thirty-three the youngest divisional commander in Hood's army, formed his division of three proven brigades southwest of the McGavock farm. The Arkansas brigade of Daniel Reynolds was on the left. These battle-tested troops were the best Walthall had. But the veteran brigade was much reduced in numbers from the hard fighting around Atlanta. More serious was the fact that Cantey's brigade had suffered from changes in leadership. The Alabama-Mississippi brigade was commanded by inexperienced Brig. Gen. Charles M. Shelley. He had never led a brigade in battle, and Walthall placed in front of Shelley the well-led brigade of William A. Quarles. Walthall hoped that by placing Quarles with Shelley in support the latter could follow without making any grave mistakes. Walthall knew that Quarles's seven Alabama and Tennessee regiments could be depended on.

Walthall's division, when it received orders to advance, threw out skirmishers in three lines. Almost immediately the skirmishers began to draw fire; so they slowed down to allow the deployed regiments to come up for closer support. The staccato bursts of rifle fire drew heavier as the advance continued. Men began to spin around and fall as bullets found their mark.

Quarles's and Shelley's lines began to move to the left, crowding Reynolds's brigade. This drift was due to Loring's lines pushing over as the course of the river changed. Walthall's lines became a little loose as the whole division stormed across the railroad.

Reilly's Union brigade was waiting with aimed guns as the Confederates surged forward. A tremendous storm of bullets met the graycoats as they made their way through the abatis fronting the works. The main body of Walthall's command melted under the murderous fire, but many rebels leaped the works and crossed bayonets with the Yankee soldiers.

Shelley, anxious to prove himself, led his troops straight for the breastworks, sword held high, the bullets somehow missing him, and leaped the ditch and got to the top with a handful of gallant men from Alabama. The crash of rifles swept the line, and when the smoke drifted away, the rebels were down except for Shelley, who made his way back to the Confederate lines.

Quarles formed his thousand men for another rush upon the breastworks. Once more there was a bitter exchange of gunfire and savage, hand-to-hand fighting. Quarles's men caught a deadly flank fire from Casement's troops. Quarles's brigade was compelled to withdraw, with Quarles wounded and half of his brigade shot down. His brigade had lost so heavily that the officer highest in rank was a captain.

Reforming under the cover of a low slope, Walthall's regiments went in again. A terrible frenzy of combat descended on the fighting line. Men were possessed by insane excitement, shouting loudly, bursting out in hysterical laughter, crowding up to fire at the Yankee line. Under all the deafening tumult there was the thud-thud of bullets tearing into human flesh.

Reilly's and Casement's rifle fire rose to a new intensity as they tried to slaughter their foes. The fire was more than the valiant men from Alabama and Tennessee could bear. The rebel lines thinned and faded back into the dark, smoky fields.

Good-soldier Reynolds reformed his Arkansas regiments carefully, and they went in bravely again, the crack troops crouching low as they advanced. The Ninth and Twenty-fifth Arkansas had moved close to the Union line when, for some unknown reason, they shifted their front and moved by the left flank away from the Union line, exposing their flanks. The Union soldiers, with bullets and grapeshot at close range, raked the flanks of the Arkansas regiments, killing hundreds of the bravest and best soldiers of Arkansas. The regiments turned and with a yell went for the earthworks, but this served only to swell the casualty list. There was another volley that tore their ranks and it was too much: the men turned and fled.

Walthall's fine brigades were a bloody mess. They had lost almost half of their total strength. Quarles's brigade alone had lost four hundred and thirty-two men out of a thousand. The story was about the same in the other two brigades. Many regiments were under captains.

On Walthall's right there was sound of firing from Loring, and the sound of battle was heavy on the left. So Walthall did as Loring, Brown, and Cleburne; he reformed his regiments and sent them back in, and it was the same story: advance and retreat, charge and countercharge against the breastworks that blazed from end to end with a crackling sheet of flame until late in the night.

Forty-five-year-old Maj. Gen. Samuel G. French, who commanded Stewart's Third Division, had commanded a division in Robert E. Lee's army but was transferred to the Army of Tennessee after he had a disagreement with Longstreet about his handling of the division. French was punctilious, precise, and imperturbable.

French was concerned about his division going into action without its third brigade of four good Texas and two North Carolina regiments under one-legged Matthew Ector. This brigade had Hood's pontoon train and was busy trying to find a suitable place for the heavy army wagons loaded with the scows, planking, and other gear.

On the Right at Franklin

French deployed his two brigades in a ragged patch of woodland along the edge of the Nashville and Decatur railroad. The two brigades would have to move down the railroad embankment to strike the Union lines. French was worried about the railroad making his lines loose.

A little past four, General French was ordered to take his division up the railroad and get into action. French, still worried, moved as ordered, and, before long from Winstead Hill, Hood could see the four parallel lines of Sam French's division moving up the track, heading for the Union earthworks.

French rode with his division and could see smoke and hear gunfire off to the left, where Wagner's men were firing on Cleburne's division, and some firing seemed to be going on to the east near the McGavock house; but in front, as far as French could see, there was nothing at all except rolling fields and the railroad track straight as an arrow.

Francis M. Cockrell's brigade stopped to allow the Mississippi brigade of Claudius Sears to come up alongside. Ector's brigade was following. French supposed it was following, at any rate. They had been told to do so after they parked the pontoon train.

French's division went north across the fields, the lines wavering as men came under artillery fire. The Union guns by the cotton gin, east of the Columbia pike, had a target so wide and solid that they could not miss. The long lines carefully aligned, battle flags flying, white smoke clouds breaking overhead here and there as shells exploded pushed on.

Over the fields, through belts of trees which ran west and east and through the felled beech trees, French's troops marched on under fire. The brigades were veering more to the left as French's troops were crowded by Walthall's regiments.

Wagner's men, in their advanced position, had driven Cleburne's brigades back, and these Yankee troops were now aiming their rifles at French's unsuspecting men just where it would hurt most—from the left.

The invisible blow came suddenly. One minute French was sitting on his horse amid the leading regiment, watching the Yankees in their main line; the next minute there was a uproar of rifle fire and screaming men in the fields to the left. Cockrell's brigade abruptly found itself under a deadly fire from the flank. Regiments broke, men ran for cover, officers shouted frantically; the brigade dissolved and the men ran back through the beech trees and into an open field, where they were caught by artillery from near the cotton gin and guns on the Union right.

Wagner's troops cheered as French's soldiers reeled back. The cheers were short-lived, for the sound of gunfire roared again as Cleburne's troops went back in. French rallied Cockrell's regiments; Sears's brigade had gotten out in good order but was shaken some by the unexpected folding of Cockrell's men.

At five o'clock French advanced again in three massive lines. This time his men met no deadly fire on the flanks since Wagner's division had been routed by other rebel brigades. French's men pressed toward the main Yankee line. Their advance so far had been rather unnerving. They had come up through the backwash of combat, seeing many wounded from Walthall's division and other ghastly debris that filled the fields.

The battle line divided as the men went by a burning barn. As the lines closed up beyond the barn, and with sharp rifle fire coming down from the earthworks, the Confederates fixed bayonets and headed for the works.

Within 1,000 yards they came; 900 it was; 800 yards. Then a hoarsely shouted command was repeated by each

Union battery commander. Almost before the orders were uttered, the lanyards were pulled. The shells of twenty guns went screaming toward the gray lines. The startled infantry of Sears's and Cockrell's brigades hesitated a moment but responded gallantly to the commands of their officers and steadfastly pushed on again. Once more, and still once more Cox's artillery tore the ranks. Still the rebels pushed on.

Sears's Mississippians charged over a part of the Union line, and they shot and stabbed at an Indiana regiment that was in behind it, and after a flurry of hand-to-hand fighting along the earthworks the rebels withdrew.

French's two brigades were fought to a standstill, but fresh troops were coming up. Ector's brigade arrived yelling and went swinging up the slope with their battle flags snapping. They came up just in time, for French's men were in serious trouble. One regiment had been broken and the rest were taking a deadly fire. Ector's men went charging for Reilly's line with savage power. Volleys echoed down the front. The Confederates answered and came on.

The Twenty-ninth and Thirty-ninth North Carolina came to grips with the enemy; the Texas regiments met a terrible shock of point-blank fire too hot for any troops. Half of the Fourteenth Texas cavalry (dismounted) regiment fell in the first volley, and all the regiment's color-bearers went down and most of the field officers. The two North Carolina regiments met fresh Union troops, and slowly they were pushed back over the barricade. Ector's brigade was finished.

French's division had been mowed down. Fire in front and enfilading blasts of Union batteries slaughtered almost half of Sears's and Cockrell's troops, and General Cockrell had been wounded. Ector's proud brigade had been reduced to seven hundred men as a result of the fire from the powerful blue regiments.

Chapter VII

The Cavalry

"Boots and Saddles" was sounded promptly for Jackson's and Buford's troopers at four o'clock or after when Forrest, in silent wrath, prepared to move against Wilson's mounted force.

Although war had swept away most of the manmade obstacles, fences, and gates and had created as fair a field as knights could have asked for a tourney, there were treacherous ditches across some of the fields near the Harpeth. Across these fields, in columns of squadrons at a trot, swept Forrest's troopers.

About four-thirty, Forrest, on the Lewisburg pike, heard the sound of firing from the direction of Hughes' Ford. He could not misunderstand the firing. The Union cavalry must be crossing the river. There could not be another explanation. Soon a dashing courier on a panting horse brought word from Abraham Buford: The Yankees were on the south side of the Harpeth at Hughes' Ford and were advancing in strong force. Forrest immediately directed that the rest of Jackson's division reinforce Buford.

Hatch and Croxton had pushed their columns across and were trying to flush Buford's men out of some woods. There was bitter fighting as the gray and blue troopers snapped at one another with carbines and pistols. The Yankees surged forward, dismounted, and sought to finish Buford's troopers. As the bluecoats rushed the rebels, those Confederates who looked from the woods in the direction of the Lewisburg pike saw a sight that made veterans catch their breath and stare and lift their hats in admiration. Jackson's regiments were coming up in magnificent order. Sweeping in splendor across the field abreast of Jackson's column was Morton's horse artillery.

Jackson diverged to the east in order to get outside the woods, and to trap the Yankees his right regiments drove across the fields. The Union troopers saw Jackson's objective, and with a gallantry that matched his, they threw themselves at him. Jackson changed his column to the left, met Croxton's troopers, made them wheel, and then, in close columns of squadrons, he swept the field. The Yankees fell back toward Hughes' Ford, in the direction of Forrest's advance with the rest of his cavalry. Immediately there was a rolling melee, confused by smoke and dust; but when this cleared, Forrest was still advancing. The Yankees, in wild confusion, were falling back across Hughes' Ford. Once across they began to form lines in the woods to contest Forrest's crossing.

As Jackson and Forrest were sweeping the Yankees across Hughes' Ford, Bell's and Lyon's dismounted brigades had been pressing along the west bank of the Harpeth and had cut off part of Hatch's division near the McGavock farm. A brief, fierce fight followed. The clang of cold steel rang across the meadows. Hatch's troopers fought their way out of the trap and made their way across the Harpeth.

Clearing the ground across the Harpeth and getting around Schofield's flank became Forrest's next tasks. This was undertaken by Buford's tough brigade. In a gallant charge across the Harpeth, with bullets emptying saddles, Buford easily drove Croxton's troopers northward.

Forrest quickly sent the rest of Jackson's division splashing across Hughes' Ford. Further north, Bell and Lyon were crossing under heavy fire. Their forces soon joined, and with a rebel yell the Confederates charged through the woods, and a furious pistol-and-carbine fight waged. The Union troopers pulled back slowly but the fight was bloody. Every inch of ground was contested. The rebels became confused in their bloody advance and had to halt to reform.

All along the line, from the east bank of the Harpeth across the fields and woods to the right, there was a lull in the cavalry fight. Forrest was not pleased with the lull. He noticed fresh Union troopers arriving on the field and knew that his men would have to go to the defense if these fresh Yankees made counterattacks.

Lyon's Kentucky brigade was especially on the alert because their position was the most vulnerable. In front of it, a little brook and some ditches gave some security. Next, defensively, was a fringe of woodland on the right where dismounted pickets were stationed. Behind this wood was a field, which rose somewhat northward, where Lyon's line of foot troopers was drawn. This line was thin and had no protection on the extreme right except two guns of Morton's horse artillery. If the flank was turned or the line broken, the right would be thrown back on the left, which might be routed. If Lyon's brigade gave way, then the rest of Forrest's mounted army would be in serious trouble.

Forrest's men could hear the heavy sound of battle from Hood's infantry on the other side of the river. The rebel troopers knew that the lull was costing them precious time. Forrest felt that the halt was effecting the outcome of the battle.

A stir in the woods and on the fields held by the Yankees was observable at five o'clock. Soon Wilson's troopers began a deliberate advance on the center and right. At first evidence of attack, Forrest called some of his staff to join him, and with them he rode to a section of Morton's artillery out in a field. By the time he got there, artillerists who had been under heavy fire were half-demoralized. Dead horses and slain comrades ringed them. Forrest ordered the guns to withdraw and directed Buford to organize a counterattack. As always, Forrest felt that the best way to defend was to attack.

Buford sent a yelling mass of seven hundred men, armed with shotguns, pistols, and carbines, charging against Harrison's fresh brigade. There was a furious hand-to-hand fight with pistols, clubbed rifles, sabers, and knives. The Confederates were repulsed with heavy loss after Harrison's men were reinforced by two regiments from Croxton.

General Forrest could see that further Confederate action was futile. Wilson had too many troops. Forrest ordered all of his troops that were still on the east side of the Harpeth to cross to the west bank and return to Hood's main army. Forrest, without all of his cavalry, could not turn Schofield's flank.

On the Confederate left, Chalmers's division was approaching the Yankee barricade from the west. In front, Biffle's advance guard had located elements of Kimball's division. Their right seemed to be in heavy woods but at a distance little could be seen. In front of the woods on the right of the road and across fields ran the tall earthworks, which evidently was defended by strong units.

Biffle scrutinized as much of this as could be seen on a quick reconnaissance, and then he turned to Chalmers and asked permission to push two dismounted squadrons as skirmishers. With his chief's approval, Biffle sent word for the squadrons to advance.

The skirmishers went forward but recoiled in front of the breastworks; Chalmers himself, with Ed Rucker's aid, rallied the contingent that had wavered. Now the Ninth Tennessee, with drawn sabers, was yelling furiously and charging straight for the breastworks in columns of fours. The column reached the works and was galloping in front of it toward the Union right. The men had drawn their pistols and were firing at the bluecoats behind the barricade, but they were not able to get over the barrier. The Ninth was forced to pull back, leaving over a hundred dead and wounded in front of the works.

Chalmers dismounted his regiments. One more charge, this time on foot, eight regiments went running across the fields toward the blazing breastworks. Biffle's troops were cut down by squadrons. Chalmers men pushed on through the sharp rifle fire, shooting their carbines and double-barreled shotguns, and then rushed forward, dodging back and forth until they came to close quarters with the Yankees. With the brim of their slouch hats falling over their foreheads and with rebel yells, the Confederates charged over the works. With both sides using clubbed rifles, bayonets, sabers, and pistols, a desperate and deadly hand-to-hand conflict ensued. The Seventh Alabama and Fifteenth Tennessee, greatly outnumbered, stubbornly fell back, leaving behind in dead and wounded many of their number.

On the opposite flank of the Confederate line, Colonel Biffle's column, reinforced by Dibrell's brigade, went again forward. A furious fire of grapeshot, canister, and exploding shell from the Yankee artillery and a galling fire from the Union infantry behind the works forced the attackers back.

The Confederate cavalry charged the Union works five times but were repulsed with heavy losses each time. The rebels would get within twenty yards of the works, and then a deadly fire would scatter the wavering lines.

Soon after six o'clock that evening, Chalmers ordered his forces to fall back to Winstead Hill where they could reform and replenish their supply of ammunition.

Forrest's cavalry, as had the infantry, fought piecemeal and drained themselves dry in futile charges. If Hood had only permitted Forrest that one division of infantry to assist the cavalry in turning Schofield's flank, then the battle would have ended in victory for the Confederacy.

Chapter VIII

The Last Attacks

Cheatham deployed William Bate's division on the extreme Confederate left. Bate, who had three brigades, had placed T. B. Smith's and Henry Jackson's brigades in the first assaulting line, with Bullock in the second.

At length, Bate received word to go in after Brown's division was out of the fight. Across the fields moved Jackson's brigade. On his left, Smith was emerging with Bullock not far behind. Soon there was a halt. Lagging units caught up. At a shouted command, the long line was dressed. A breeze lifted the smoke and seventeen battle flags began to flap.

Soon the lines passed Cheatham. Salutes were exchanged. Cheatham looked with admiration as his third division stepped forward. Bate halted briefly in a little depression south of the Bostick house. Presstman's battery had limbered up and was following Bate. The lines waited while Presstman unlimbered in the Bostick yard with shells bursting all around. The brigades went steadfastly into the full fury of Ruger's fire.

Bate's troops, taking the fire of the batteries, charged into canister with a yell; they defied it; they kept straight on. Moore's Yankees gave way to fire at will. Every man loaded and rammed and pulled the trigger as fast as he could. Many a Union minié ball found its mark, and many Confederates fell under the artillery fire; but there was no halting now. Rebel blood was up. The front line pushed on to the works. Jackson's Georgia brigade was at grips with the Union defenders.

Farther west, the Florida brigade of Brigadier General Bullock got into a tremendous series of fights around the earthworks, captured them, lost them, recaptured them and lost them again, and then was blasted out for good by two Union batteries that had been rolled up to the works. The Florida brigade retired with a loss of two-thirds of its number.

Bate's Confederates paused for breath and realignment, and then sent a powerful column straight in on the low earthworks. Moore's men held their fire until the range suited them, and the men from Michigan and Ohio put in a wrecking fire. The whole front rank of Bate's line seemed to go down in smoke and dust, but there were other lines that kept on coming, and the Union guns took their toll.

Some of T. B. Smith's men found shelter in a muddy ravine that ran in front of the Union line. Smith packed two regiments in and began volleying away at the Yankees.

Presstman's battery was hurting the Yankees. Far-off to the left, beyond the Carter house, Schofield's long-range guns came into action, hitting hard at the rebel guns by the Bostick house. Presstman's men began to take a frightful pounding. Caissons were blown up, gun wheels were broken, men and horses were killed, and the dead and wounded were torn apart afresh by the shot and shell. Presstman had to withdraw his battered guns.

Jackson lined up the Sixty-sixth and Twenty-fifth Georgia for another try; the Thirtieth Georgia was placed on the ground to give a covering fire for the two regiments. Their battle flags waving at the head of the column, the Georgians

The Last Attacks

came up over a small rise and ran full-tilt for the breastworks, men falling at every step as bullets and shells slashed the column; there was a wild chaos of flame, smoke, and thunderous noise.

The Yankees were only twenty-five yards away and made every shot count. The colonel of one of the Georgia regiments got to the earthworks and stood there amid the bullets, one hand on the earthworks, waving his hat in large circles and yelling commands. The men surged past him and engaged in a flurry of hand-to-hand fighting.

The Yankees stood their ground. Nearly half of the Sixty-sixth Georgia was down; ammunition was almost gone. The Twenty-fifth Georgia broke, leaving a dense carpet of dead and wounded on the ground. Broken waves of Georgians were going back toward Winstead Hill. The rest of the men from Georgia who did not run were captured or slain.

Smith's brigade made another valiant charge. For a while there was a furious exchange from stationary lines. Then slowly, but with supreme resolution, the Thirty-seventh Georgia began to advance with three Tennessee regiments in support.

Every step of ground was contested, but Smith's troops stormed the earthworks and grappled with the Yankees. Just after taking the works, a heavy column of Union infantry appeared on Smith's right, and another strong column advanced upon Smith's rear. The Georgians and Tennesseans wheeled around with cheers, abandoning the Union works and literally cutting their way out with bayonets, but they lost many men, including Capt. Tod Carter, who fell mortally wounded almost in his father's yard.

Major General Edward Johnson's division of Lee's corps prepared to go into action. Johnson's division had arrived after the first assault had started and had been held in reserve. Hood, upon hearing the slackening of the firing, decided to order Johnson's men to attack. The rest of Lee's corps—Clayton's and Stevenson's divisions—did not arrive on the field until the battle was over.

Tall and slim Edward Johnson, called "Old Allegheny" by his men, brought forward his four veteran brigades. His troops were hard-hitting and had confidence in Johnson. He got his soldiers near the Bostick house and formed them into four lines in the murk of the fading day, and it seemed to him that the best chance was to keep going without a halt. If the rebels ever stopped to fire they were lost; it was best to make a straight, cold-steel charge out of it. He issued his orders accordingly, his veterans fixed bayonets, and forward they went through the human debris of the previous charges. The wounded men on the ground reached up and tried to hold them back, telling them it was suicide to go on. It was nearly dark, the field was muddy, and the Confederates stumbled on through the dead and wounded and the clutching hands of the unwounded and wounded, and their lines grew disordered. General Manigault galloped up, sword swinging in the dim light, yelling to the men to close and dress their ranks. Just then a great sheet of fire lit up the entire length of the earthworks and farther back quick flashings from Yankee cannon. General Manigault was shot down and so was nearly a fourth of the division. The men staggered to a halt and fired a ragged volley or two. Then they gave way as all the others had done and went streaming back to the Bostick house.

It was entirely dark when Jacob Sharp's Mississippi brigade from Johnson's division made one final assault, coming up from the ravine and swinging out into the open ground comparatively undamaged, and then getting the worst of it in one tremendous, tearing blast that seemed to wipe out entire regiments. Sharp's men pushed toward the breastworks, in spite of Union artillery and infantry fire. The Southern troops were fortunate, as the lead from thousands of small arms and numerous fragments of shell broke around them, the smoke and the merciful darkness covering the human targets. Casualties were not heavy as the shouting Confederates climbed the earthworks. Prisoners were taken and told to make their way to the rear. Sharp's brigade had the works and there was no support for them. Sharp had his men straighten their lines to wait for the expected support.

For a few minutes there was silence, but for a few minutes only. Through the shadows the Confederates could see a heavy mass of infantry north of them. The rumble of many voices was audible. Strong lines were advancing. The Confederates did not know whether they were Yankee or rebel. Sharp had been cautioned to watch for support on either flank and in front, because Deas or Manigault might storm the works before he got there. The powerful, advancing line might belong to one of them. As Sharp questioned, a heavy fire swept along the front of the approaching troops. Sharp did not reply. The fire might have come from Confederates who mistook his men for Yankees. Another volley—screams and the oaths of wounded men. Still Sharp did not fire. A third volley! This volley was so near that the flash of the rifles lit the uniforms of the soldiers: they were blue.

General Sharp gave them every bullet he had in the rifles of his brigade. For a moment, firing fast, he held them at bay. Soon he saw a second line behind the first. In rear of the second line was another line. To these odds he could oppose no troops except those of his own. Further resistance would be futile. Sharp withdrew his brigade back across the dark, smoky fields.

The battle of November 30 now was ended. Schofield, shocked by Hood's insanity, gave order to his men to start retreating at eleven o'clock, and by midnight they deserted the earthworks they had so vigorously defended, and moved across the Harpeth and on the highway to Nashville so silently that the exhausted Confederates did not know that they had gone. A house caught fire during the retreat, frightening the Union commanders, but it failed to reveal the movement of their army to the Confederates.

Chapter IX

The Aftermath

Hood's artillery, which had arrived during the night, fired into the Union works on the morning of December 1. There was no reply—Schofield's army was gone. The rounds fired by the Confederates served only as a salute to the dead.

As Hood's troops went down the Columbia pike, they were dazed by the human wreckage they saw. On their right, where Cleburne's troops fought, they found bodies dreadfully broken and dismembered from artillery. In places where infantry fire had been especially intense the dead rebels lay in great rows. An Alabama soldier wrote: "As far as the eye could see on both sides of the Columbia pike, you see gray-coated boys, swollen up, quite black in the face with staring eyes."

Confederates who had been in the thickest of the fighting were shocked when they went about the field and saw how terrible the killing had really been. On that field of carnage, one rebel officer counted more than three hundred dead Confederates in a four-hundred-foot stretch of the ditch near the Carter house.

Worst of all was along the railroad cut near the Lewisburg pike where Loring's division had fought. The cut was festooned with corpses. In front of the line, where Casement's brigade had been, the dead soldiers were piled on top of one another, and it seemed as if whole regiments had gone down in regular ranks.

Cheatham's corps was hardly as big as a division. His corps had lost more than a third of its men, and its best generals—Cleburne, Gist, Strahl, and Granbury—were dead. Brown would be out for months. Stewart's corps had suffered nearly as much. Some of the army's finest combat units had been all but destroyed—Strahl's brigade, the Twentieth Tennessee, the Thirty-third Alabama, the Ninth Texas, and the Twenty-fifth Georgia. The infantry losses had been so heavy that Hood had to consolidate many of his best regiments. Eleven of the twenty-nine brigades were under temporary commanders.

Great fires were built to consume the carcasses of dead horses. Burial details were at work over the fields, collecting and burying the slain. Long, wide trenches were dug for mass burial. The stiff bodies were laid in them side by side, then another layer, as if stacking cordwood. Hood said they buried one thousand but the count seems to have been too low. In hundreds of cases no identification was possible, and the men went into the ground as "Unknown." In places burial details missed bodies for the burial trench and simply shoveled earth over them as they lay on the ground.

The country town of Franklin had been presented with some five thousand wounded rebels, and the fields and the ditches, barns, homes and churches were where they lay. So appalling was the number of men awaiting attention that Hood's overworked doctors had begun with a grim job of sorting, separating men who were bound to die from those whose lives might be saved. The doctors worked feverishly, cutting off arms and legs, with an army wagon hauling off the limbs and hurrying back for another load. Hood's medical service frantically wired Beauregard to have Richmond ship alcohol, nitric acid, tin cups, buckets, bed sacks, and other equipment to Franklin.

On the long, back gallery of the McGavock house, the

bodies of Cleburne, Adams, Gist, Strahl, and Granbury were laid out side by side. The officers had died upon the field in such large numbers that Hood's officer's corps was ruined. In addition to five generals, six colonels, two lieutenant colonels, three majors, and two captains were killed. Fifteen colonels, nine lieutenant colonels, six majors, and three captains were wounded. Two colonels, two majors, and four captains were missing in action. Over twelve hundred enlisted men were slain. Dry statistics, yes, but when we remember that these figures represent men killed or wounded, citizens lost to the southern part of the nation, and, not only that, but the loss of the sons that should have been born to these slaughtered men, every sentence acquires a deep, mournful interest. We can be proud of American valor, but we should also be humiliated by the supreme folly of civil war.

Slowly, and with immense effort, the shot-to-pieces ghost of an army pulled itself together and took to the road heading north toward Nashville in expectation of a new battle with Lee's corps out front, since it had suffered little in the battle and had rested from its prodigious hike from Columbia. It was not an army now, but merely the spirit of an army. Never again, after Franklin, was the Army of Tennessee to be an formidable force in battle because the army died at Franklin.

Appendix

Organization of the Army of Tennessee during the Tennessee campaign, as of November 1, 1864.

CHEATHAM'S CORPS
Maj. Gen. Benjamin F. Cheatham

Brown's Division
Maj. Gen. John C. Brown

Gist's Brigade:
Brig. Gen. States Rights Gist
46th Georgia Regiment
65th Georgia Regiment
16th South Carolina Regiment
24th South Carolina Regiment

Maney's Brigade:
Brig. Gen. John C. Carter
4th Tennessee Regiment
6th Tennessee Regiment
9th Tennessee Regiment
50th Tennessee Regiment
1st Tennessee Regiment
27th Tennessee Regiment
8th Tennessee Regiment

16th Tennessee Regiment
28th Tennessee Regiment

Strahl's Brigade:
Brig. Gen. O. F. Strahl
4th Tennessee Regiment
5th Tennessee Regiment
31st Tennessee Regiment
33d Tennessee Regiment
38th Tennessee Regiment
19th Tennessee Regiment
24th Tennessee Regiment
41st Tennessee Regiment

Vaughan's Brigade:
Brig. Gen. George W. Gordon
11th Tennessee Regiment
12th Tennessee Regiment
13th Tennessee Regiment
29th Tennessee Regiment
47th Tennessee Regiment
51st Tennessee Regiment
52d Tennessee Regiment
154th Tennessee Regiment

Bate's Division
Maj. Gen. William B. Bate

Tyler's Brigade:
Brig. Gen. Thomas Smith (?)
37th Georgia Regiment
4th Georgia Sharpshooters
2d Tennessee Regiment

10th Tennessee Regiment
20th Tennessee Regiment
37th Tennessee Regiment

Jackson's Brigade:
Brig. Gen. Henry R. Jackson
1st Georgia Regiment
66th Georgia Regiment
25th Georgia Regiment
29th Georgia Regiment
30th Georgia Regiment
1st Georgia Sharpshooters

Finley's Brigade:
Brig. Gen. Bullock
1st Florida Regiment
3d Florida Regiment
6th Florida Regiment
7th Florida Regiment
4th Florida Regiment
1st Florida (dismounted)
   Cavalry Regiment

Cleburne's Division
Maj. Gen. Pat Cleburne

Govan's Brigade:
Brig. Gen. Daniel C. Govan
1st Arkansas Regiment
2d Arkansas Regiment
5th Arkansas Regiment
13th Arkansas Regiment
15th Arkansas Regiment
24th Arkansas Regiment

6th Arkansas Regiment
7th Arkansas Regiment
8th Arkansas Regiment
19th Arkansas Regiment

Smith's Brigade:
Brig. Gen. T. B. Smith
(Regiments Unknown)

Lowrey's Brigade:
Brig. Gen. Mark Lowrey
16th Alabama Regiment
33d Alabama Regiment
45th Alabama Regiment
5th Mississippi Battalion
3d Mississippi Battalion
8th Mississippi Regiment
32d Mississippi Regiment

Granbury's Brigade:
   Brig. Gen. H. B. Granbury
   35th Tennessee Regiment
   6th Texas Regiment
   15th Texas Regiment
   7th Texas Regiment
   10th Texas Regiment
* 17th Cav. Regiment (dismounted)
* 18th Cav. Regiment (dismounted)
* 24th Cav. Regiment (dismounted)
* 25th Cav. Regiment (dismounted)

---

*All Texas Cavalry Regiments

Appendix

LEE'S CORPS
Lieut. Gen. Stephen D. Lee

Johnson's Division

Maj. Gen. Edward Johnson

Deas's Brigade:
Brig. Gen. Zachariah C. Deas
19th Alabama Regiment
22th Alabama Regiment
25th Alabama Regiment
39th Alabama Regiment
50th Alabama Regiment

Manigault's Brigade:
Brig. Gen. A. M. Manigault
24th Alabama Regiment
28th Alabama Regiment
10th South Carolina Regiment
19th South Carolina Regiment
34th Alabama Regiment

Brantley's Brigade:
Brig. Gen. William Brantley
24th Mississippi Regiment
34th Mississippi Regiment
27th Mississippi Regiment
29th Mississippi Regiment
30th Mississippi Regiment

Sharp's Brigade:
Brig. Gen. Jacob H. Sharp
7th Mississippi Regiment

9th Mississippi Regiment
10th Mississippi Regiment
44th Mississippi Regiment
41st Mississippi Regiment

Cantey's Brigade:
(Commander Unknown)
17th Alabama Regiment
26th Alabama Regiment
29th Alabama Regiment
37th Mississippi Regiment

Stevenson's Division
Maj. Gen. Carter L. Stevenson

Pettus's Brigade:
Brig. Gen. Edmund W. Pettus
20th Alabama Regiment
23d Alabama Regiment
30th Alabama Regiment
31st Alabama Regiment
46th Alabama Regiment

Cumming's Brigade:
(Commander not known)
34th Georgia Regiment
36th Georgia Regiment
39th Georgia Regiment
56th Georgia Regiment

Clayton's Division
Maj. Gen. Henry D. Clayton

Gibson's Brigade:
Brig. Gen. Randall L. Gibson

Appendix

1st Louisiana Regiment
4th Louisiana Regiment
13th Louisiana Regiment
16th Louisiana Regiment
19th Louisiana Regiment
20th Louisiana Regiment
30th Louisiana Regiment

Stovall's Brigade:
Brig. Gen. Marcellus A. Stovall
40th Georgia Regiment
41st Georgia Regiment
42d Georgia Regiment
43d Georgia Regiment
52d Georgia Regiment

Holtzclaw's Brigade:
Brig. Gen. James Holtzclaw
18th Alabama Regiment
32th Alabama Regiment
58th Alabama Regiment
36th Alabama Regiment
38th Alabama Regiment

ARTILLERY
LEE'S CORPS

Johnston's Battalion—Two Georgia, one Tennessee battery
Courtney's Battalion—Two Alabama, one Texas battery
Eldridge's Battalion—Two Alabama, one Mississippi, one Louisiana battery

STEWART'S CORPS
Lieut. Gen. Alexander P. Stewart

Loring's Division
Maj. Gen. William W. Loring

Featherston's Brigade:
Brig. Gen. Winfield S. Featherston
1st Mississippi Regiment
3d Mississippi Regiment
22d Mississippi Regiment
31st Mississippi Regiment
33d Mississippi Regiment
40th Mississippi Regiment

Scott's Brigade:
Brig. Gen. John S. Scott
55th Alabama Regiment
57th Alabama Regiment
27th Alabama Regiment
35th Alabama Regiment
49th Alabama Regiment
12th Louisiana Regiment

Adams's Brigade:
Brig. Gen. John Adams
6th Mississippi Regiment
14th Mississippi Regiment
15th Mississippi Regiment
20th Mississippi Regiment
23d Mississippi Regiment
43d Mississippi Regiment

ARTILLERY
STEWART'S CORPS

Truehart's Battalion—Three Alabama batteries
Myrick's Battalion—One Louisiana, two Mississippi batteries
Storr's Battalion—One Missouri, one Mississippi, one Alabama battery

CHEATHAM'S CORPS

Hoxton's Battalion—One Florida, one Alabama, one Mississippi battery
Hotchkiss's Battalion—One Missouri, one Alabama, one

French's Division
Maj. Gen. Samuel G. French

Ector's Brigade.
Brig. Gen. M. D. Ector
29th North Carolina Regiment
39th North Carolina Regiment
9th Texas Regiment
10th Texas (dismounted) Cavalry Regiment
14th Texas (dismounted) Cavalry Regiment
32d Texas (dismounted) Cavalry Regiment

Cockrell's Brigade:
Brig. Gen. F. M. Cockrell

Sear's Brigade:
Brig. Gen. Claudius Sears
4th Mississippi Regiment
35th Mississippi Regiment
36th Mississippi Regiment
39th Mississippi Regiment
46th Mississippi Regiment

Walthall's Division
Maj. Gen. Edward C. Walthall

Quarles's Brigade:
Brig. Gen. William A. Quarles
1st Alabama Regiment
42d Tennessee Regiment
46th Tennessee Regiment
49th Tennessee Regiment
53d Tennessee Regiment
55th Tennessee Regiment
48th Tennessee Regiment

Reynolds's Brigade:
Brig. Gen. Daniel H. Reynolds
4th Arkansas Regiment
9th Arkansas Regiment
25th Arkansas Regiment

Arkansas battery
Cobb's Battalion—One South Carolina, one Tennessee, one Louisiana battery

CAVALRY
Maj. Gen. Nathan B. Forrest

Two Cavalry divisions—Brig. Gen. Chalmer's and Jackson's. Approximately 8,000 troopers—Units not known
Total aggregate strength: infantry, artillery and cavalry: 40,000

Bibliography

Clark, Charles T. *Opdyke Tigers: 125th Ohio Volunteer Infantry.* Columbus, 1895
Cox, Jacob D. *The Battle of Franklin.* New York, 1897.
Dyer, John P. *The Gallant Hood.* Indianapolis, 1950.
Freeman, Douglas Southall. *Lee's Lieutenants.* 3 vols. New York, 1942.
Hay, Thomas R. *Hood's Tennessee Campaign.* New York, 1929.
Henry, Robert S. *The Story of the Confederacy.* Indianapolis, 1931.
Hood, John B. *Advance and Retreat.* New Orleans, 1880.
Horn, Stanley F. *The Army of Tennessee.* Indianapolis, 1941.
―――― *Tennessee Historical Quarterly.* Volume XIV, number 4. December, 1955.
Van Horne, Thomas B. *The Life of General George H. Thomas.* New York, 1882
―――― *War of the Rebellion; Official Records of the Union and Confederate Armies.* XLV. Washington, 1880-1901.